Praise for *Hope in*

The scope and depth of this work is breathtak~~...~~ in Andy's words is simultaneously soothing an~~...~~ heart of addiction on both a global and personal level, indicting systems and exposing the heart, while equally offering profound hope for those who suffer addiction, and for those who love those who war with desire. This is a brilliant gift from a man called to the margins whose passion offers us all a taste of the One whose presence is what we truly desire.

DAN B. ALLENDER, PHD, professor of counseling psychology and founding president, The Seattle School of Theology and Psychology

If I had to choose one book to hand someone struggling to understand the power of addiction in their own life or in the life of a loved one, this would be it. Andy Partington's book combines the best scholarly insight on addiction with hard-won pastoral wisdom, and it's all narratively displayed in a series of gripping stories of addiction and recovery and the communities that make both possible. Clear, wise, compassionate, and completely engaging.

KENT DUNNINGTON, PHD, professor of philosophy, Biola University, and author of *Addiction and Virtue*

Addiction is the real pandemic of our time and is no respecter of culture or borders. What is addiction? How can we describe it? What are its causes and its effects on family and society? Are there any viable solutions? Is there any hope for those clutched in addiction's grip? This inspired book by Andy Partington wrestles with these questions and more. Through storytelling, statistical research, and personal experience, Andy helps us all come to grips with the causes and cures of addiction and the role the church can play. I wholeheartedly recommend this as must-read material!

TOM BREMER, MA, LPC, director, Europe Teen Challenge

Too many of us look for the right program, the right prayer, the right person to solve a problem, rather than accepting that addiction is complex. In *Hope in Addiction*, Andy Partington addresses the roots of addiction, the personal experiences and societal conditions that have made us vulnerable to addiction—and offers hope for change. This hope, however, is for the long haul, not the quick fix. With a heart of compassion, Andy delivers wisdom gained from years of experience working in addiction recovery as well as current research that gives us critical insight into the sources and strength of addiction. Read it all! The US is a nation of addictions—the future of ministry must include an informed, compassionate approach to recovery.

DEBORAH BEDDOE, author of *The Heart of Recovery: How Compassion and Community Offer Hope in the Wake of Addiction*

Hope in Addiction is a wake-up call for the church to address one of the greatest crises of our day: addiction. With compassion, insight, and years of practical experience, Andy Partington shows a way of hope amid this devastating and deadly crisis. This book is a must-read for faith leaders and families trying to understand and respond to the complex challenge of addiction in our midst.

TIMOTHY MCMAHAN KING, author of *Addiction Nation: What the Opioid Crisis Reveals about Us*

Gambling addiction is a huge driver of poverty, suicide, and relationship breakdown. Addictions of all kinds shatter dreams, fracture families, and destroy lives. *Hope in Addiction* brings clarity and compassion to a tough, complex subject. It sheds light on dark places. Best of all, it points us to hope—living hope!—for an addicted world.

DR. JOHN KIRKBY, CBE, founder, Christians Against Poverty (CAP)

Despair is often a word associated with our growing global addiction crisis, but this book is full of hope—not a naïve or uncertain hope, but a contagious hope that is grounded in credible research, personal experience, and, above all, a God who is at work in the world and making all things new. This is good news for everyone. In this informative, challenging, moving, and compelling memoir, Andy invites us to look beyond dominant narratives and perceptions of addiction and enter a better story. I could not recommend this book more highly.

PAUL WOOLLEY, Chief Executive, the London Institute for Contemporary Christianity (LICC)

Hope in Addiction is a hugely significant call to action for the church and wider Christian community in this current age of addiction. Andy Partington helps us understand the "why" of addiction in a way that challenges us to do more, and better, as we walk alongside those who are battling and recovering from all kinds of dependencies. The stark reality of the despair of addiction is balanced with the stories that he shares of those at different stages in their recovery journeys—encouraging us that healing and transformation is possible.

TREFLYN LLOYD-ROBERTS, General Secretary, International Substance Abuse and Addiction Coalition (ISAAC)

This book is highly detailed, well-researched, and based on years of experience and learning. It will educate and enlighten anyone who has a desire to understand addiction with its causes and its power over people. In a world of loneliness and darkness, where many are searching for purpose and meaning, this book offers hope that is found in the gospel of Christ.

STUART BELL, Senior Pastor, Alive Church, Lincoln (UK), and founding leader of the Ground Level Network

Andy Partington is a gifted storyteller able to share from his own roots in Recovery Ministry and his frontline insights in a way that invites us all to suit up and show up once more as the body of Christ in service to a dying world.

JEAN LACOUR, Founder/CEO, NET Institute and International Center for Addiction & Recovery Education (ICARE)

Andy is an Englishman and I am an American. Yet I must confess that I have learned more about the present tragic plague of addiction in the US reading *Hope in Addiction* than I have from any other book or article in recent years. Read *Hope in Addiction*. It will soften your heart, open your eyes, and minister hope to the addicted and to those who want to help the addicted.

ELLIOTT TEPPER, International Director, Betel International

I love this book because it marries the logic of the social sciences and the devotion of Christian spirituality into a compassionate intellectuality that is powerful enough to confront our terrifying addiction problems. I think that both Christians and nonbelievers, like myself, will take it to heart.

BRUCE K. ALEXANDER, PHD, Professor Emeritus of Psychology, Simon Fraser University, and author of *The Globalization of Addiction*

If you want to understand addiction, I'd read this book. If you want something more—if you want HOPE—read it slowly and carefully. You will not be disappointed!

JOHN ELDREDGE, *New York Times* bestselling author, counselor, and teacher

In an eloquent and engaging style, Andy Partington takes us through the roots of addiction and into the depth of the human predicament, before pointing us to ever-present hope. The addiction recovery movement puts us in touch with this hope, which is not just togetherness in the present, but an eternal hope found in God's presence.

EHAB EL KHARRAT, MD, PhD, founder and director, Freedom Egypt

I have the privilege of pastoring a church that has both members and staff who have found freedom from addiction through a recovery community led by Andy. His expertise doesn't just come through extensive research and study but also through years of practical experience where his understanding has been tested and refined. You won't find a better-written, clearer, or more practical guide to addiction and the routes to finding freedom from it. I thoroughly recommend it.

SIMON BENHAM, Senior Pastor, Kerith Community Church, Bracknell (UK)

Addiction to drugs and alcohol, and to various activities such as gambling, has increased markedly in recent times, in large part due to the toxic nature of modern Western capitalist society. Andy Partington takes us on a journey of discovery into the nature of addiction and recovery from addiction, introducing us to moving personal stories of hope and leading research findings that educate and inspire. This insightful and thought-provoking book contains a call to action to the church—its leaders, members, and educators. Six ways forward are proposed. This call to action is relevant to us all, since we can all contribute to the creation of transformational communities that offer hope, healing, and wholeness.

DAVID CLARK, PHD, professor emeritus of psychology, and addiction recovery advocate

Addiction is a confusing and misunderstood phenomenon. Society is generally misinformed and tied to many myths regarding the causes and mechanics of addiction. *Hope in Addiction* gets to the heart of the matter, dispelling falsehoods and opening our eyes to the actual pathology of the disease. Andy Partington does a masterful job of explaining the many aspects of addiction in such a way that the reader finds themselves thinking "aha" throughout. He explains the underlying causes including the importance of understanding the supply versus demand side as well as some new science regarding the role of dopamine in the brain. There is hope in addiction. Every faith community needs to read this book to really understand the problem and how they can play a vital role in saving lives during this "age of addiction."

REV. DR. ED TREAT, Executive Director and Founder, Center of Addiction & Faith

This is an urgent book. Andy Partington presents a well-researched and compelling case for the complex roots of addiction that steers us away from a simplistic medical or moral model. He helps us understand the contributions of early childhood trauma, despair, disconnection, isolation, yearning, and broken relationships in the volatile mix that lead us toward these surrogate yet destructive comforts, be they drugs, alcohol, or lifestyle addictions. Thankfully, this book does not leave us floundering in a hopeless state. Recovery is possible. But recovery takes comprehensive work, patience, policy changes, and supportive communities. Partington works through some practicalities of what churches can do while acknowledging that each community's response needs to be locally contextualized. But he does not shy away from insisting that what addicts need—what we all need—is spiritual community that draws us deeply into intimacy with God and one another.

AARON WHITE, author of *Recovering: From Brokenness and Addiction to Blessedness and Community*

HOPE IN ADDICTION

Understanding and Helping
Those Caught in Its Grip

ANDY PARTINGTON

MOODY PUBLISHERS

CHICAGO

Edited by Philip F. Newman
Interior design: Ragont Design
Cover design: Darren Welch
Cover illustration of paper texture copyright © 2022 by Robert Plociennik/ Shutterstock (121814140). All rights reserved.
Cover photo of grunge texture copyright © 2022 by ilolab/Shutterstock (65478910). All rights reserved.

ISBN: 978-0-8024-2328-3

Originally delivered by fleets of horse-drawn wagons, the affordable paperbacks from D. L. Moody's publishing house resourced the church and served everyday people. Now, after more than 125 years of publishing and ministry, Moody Publishers' mission remains the same—even if our delivery systems have changed a bit. For more information on other books (and resources) created from a biblical perspective, go to www.moodypublishers.com or write to:

Moody Publishers
820 N. LaSalle Boulevard
Chicago, IL 60610

1 3 5 7 9 10 8 6 4 2

Printed in the United States of America

To Daniel, Jemimah, Phoebe, JJ, and Miah.
I'm so proud of you.

Contents

Foreword

Hope in Addiction provides a proven guide to church leaders and families facing the immense challenges of wisely helping those trapped in addiction. I wrote this foreword to Andy's important book together with Brian Brunson, the recovery pastor at our church. As a senior pastor in today's culture, addressing addictions is essential to ministering to emerging generations. I wanted you to hear from both of us why Andy's book is an essential resource for all church leaders and families facing addiction.

Twenty-five years ago, my wife and I started Gateway Church to reach a generation of people who felt church was disconnected from their real lives and struggles. Our motto was "No Perfect People Allowed." We wanted to create a "Come as you are" culture in the church so that people far from God could experience the grace of God and learn to trust Him toward healing and transformation. We were amazed as thousands of people found faith in Jesus, and we were at first shocked to discover how many of them struggled with addictions. Through these people, I came to realize that the pathway out of addiction is really a biblical spiritual formation path every Christian needs.

The Recovery movement was on to something when they said that at the root of every addiction is an addiction to self—"my will be done!" I worked through the steps of recovery for my own addiction to self, and I was shocked to discover a newfound joy and experience of God's Spirit like I hadn't before. Since those first days, openly addressing addictions and the need for honesty, community, and a path forward toward recovery has been an essential part of our church. After writing *No Perfect People Allowed*, I had the privilege of speaking about creating a healing culture to church leaders in thirty countries. I was introduced to Andy's important work while speaking in the UK, and I can attest to what Andy says: addiction is truly a global epidemic we all face.

As church leaders, we cannot afford to ignore the prevalence of addiction lurking in our churches. Jesus' mission was to proclaim release for the captives, and we have the opportunity to help people in our churches and communities around us find freedom from addiction. Andy provides a wealth of experience after years in the trenches, working in addiction treatment and local church ministry in the UK and Bolivia, including founding Novō Communities. His experience creating healing communities across cultures is invaluable for all church leaders, whether you are a senior pastor, recovery pastor, or lay leader. This book will help you understand the mechanisms and roots of addiction and the critical elements of an effective recovery culture.

I (Brian) would add that Andy brings a unique perspective to the world of addiction. As a recovering addict of fifteen years, a licensed professional counselor, and a pastor working with those in addiction, I find *Hope in Addiction* a timely, valuable resource. Churches and families need guidance in creating safe, grace-filled, and restorative environments for those battling addiction. *Hope in Addiction* provides just that.

Through the pages of the book, Andy takes the reader on a journey identifying key contributors that have played a role in establishing addiction in our towns and cities. The research Andy presents comes to life as he shares the stories of so many he has journeyed with or interviewed. Real-life stories provide a valuable picture of addiction and recovery in action.

For all of us, it is vital to remember that "addiction is not an 'out there' issue." Andy appeals to churches to recognize that the agent of addiction has broken through the church's doors and is around us, whether we realize it or not. Taking a step past denial, he reminds us that "addiction is a feature of our missional context, an aspect of our cultures that we need to recognize, interpret, and engage."

After addressing the underlying causes of addiction, the book unpacks potential drivers that sustain addiction. Understanding how addiction works is critical for responding to this crisis in helpful rather than enabling ways. Andy keenly points out that there is no one-size-fits-all program. Instead, he provides a toolbox of options, based on his experience, that will assist an individual or church to begin the process of engaging, rather than avoiding, the battle for people's souls all around us.

Though there are no shortcuts, the church has the opportunity to take the necessary steps to be both preventative and responsive in our actions. We can become, as Andy encourages, "communities that are crucibles of spiritual, emotional, relational, and physical flourishing in a world of addiction."

I (John) would finally say, don't be afraid of the mess! As Andy helps us understand, it is messy creating a culture and pathway in your church to set people free. But remember, that's what Jesus did. He entered into the mess of humanity to lead us through to freedom. So, don't fear the mess. Follow Jesus into the mess, for the mess is where God's grace grows us best.

JOHN BURKE, *New York Times* bestselling author of *Imagine Heaven* and *No Perfect People Allowed*

BRIAN BRUNSON, LPC and Gateway Church Restore and Recovery Pastor

Introduction

ON THE
SHADOW SIDE

ESCAPE LADDER

Hey man, what you doin' here? You makin' people nervous."
The man asking the question was in his late fifties wearing
a black fedora. He said his name was Charles. Smooth and
assured, Charles had the presence and piercing eyes of someone high
up the food chain; of someone who, despite his smile, expected to
have his question answered. It was dusk, and I'd spent the last couple
of hours in LA's Skid Row wandering the streets and watching life
play out.

It was on the corner of Fifth and Wall Streets that Charles came
over—an envoy for the dealers who work that section of Skid Row. In
fairness, I'd been standing there a while. We talked a bit. I reassured
him I wasn't a cop—a truth betrayed by my British accent—and he
told me he'd arrived in Skid Row from Philadelphia some years back
for reasons he seemed reluctant to disclose. The conversation dried

up, so we shook hands, and sensing it was time to move on, I found a different place to stand. I hate making crack dealers nervous.

I met Smooth Charles having walked the nine blocks to Skid Row from my high-rise hotel, with its spectacular view of the Los Angeles skyline, to worship at Row Church, a "church without walls" led by Pastor Cue, a rapper turned pastor, activist, and organizer. That short walk was the final leg of an unsettling journey searching for insight into America's addiction problem. A journey that took me back and forth between the American dream and the restless purgatory on its shadow side. That morning I'd driven out of LA, through Beverly Hills, and on to Bel Air, where I couldn't help but be impressed by the spectacular hillside mansions with expansive views of the city below. From there, I drove on to Malibu, where I walked on golden sand and admired more stunning homes and perfect vistas—perfect but for the sea-bound smog, visible to both north and south, drifting out from the city. A reminder that, for all that is beautiful, all is not well in this corner of the world.

And all is not well. Walking the streets of downtown LA, you encounter the addicted, the homeless, and the untreated mentally ill on every street. Stepping into Skid Row, you step across a threshold, from outer to inner court, and into a dystopian community that the angels seem long since to have left behind. An estimated eight thousand men, women, and children live on the streets of Skid Row,[1] just a fraction of the two hundred thousand who sleep rough each night across the United States.[2] There are tents everywhere—tents and shopping carts. The shopping carts overflow with what most people call *trash*, but these citizens call *home*.

I encountered similar contradictions a half day's drive from LA in Las Vegas. Late one afternoon, I saw children, hair matted and clothes dirty, filing through the gates of the Rescue Mission's night shelter. I saw tables set, as they are each day, for 1,100 dinner guests. The Rescue Mission is a lighthouse for the city's homeless population, but talking to those who lead its work you realize that, despite gambling revenues on The Strip of $7 billion in 2021,[3] there is little help for those who reach the end of themselves.

On the other side of the country, in Huntington, West Virginia, there is a different paradox to explain. Huntington's streets are lined with churches, more than three hundred of them. It's home to a proud university and two large hospitals. Not wealthy by national standards, Huntington is a city blessed with a sense of history and shared identity foreign to many from large cities. And yet, in 2019, there were 878 reported overdoses in Huntington. Today, an estimated 10 to 20 percent of Huntington's population is in active addiction.[4]

What does it mean to be the church in a place where the death grip of addiction is so tight and unyielding?

Back in LA, Pastor Cue wrapped up the service, and a simple meal was served. I spotted Smooth Charles across the street and went over to him. "Do you want something to eat?" I asked. He didn't, so I said goodbye and began the short walk back to the dream side of the city. A soundtrack of soul, R&B, and hip-hop played all over Skid Row, and after just a few steps, I came across a group sitting around a fire, smoking, and listening to music. I smiled and said a prayer for Charles as I passed. Their track? Sade's "Smooth Operator."

As I continued my walk back toward more familiar territory, two questions occupied my mind. The first was a *why* question. Why does a place like Skid Row exist? Why is it growing? The answers are complex and multilayered, but, without a doubt, addiction is central to any explanation. Addiction is tightly woven into the torn fabric of this community, alongside mental illness, prostitution, malnutrition, poverty, and sickness. The second question was a *what* question. What does it mean to be the church, to live as followers of Jesus, in a place where the death grip of addiction is so tight and unyielding?

And not just here but also where I'm going and where you live, communities where the addiction problem may be less concentrated but the suffering no less real.

As I reflected on that question, my attention was drawn to an old wrought iron fire escape clinging to the side of one of LA's downtown, red-brick tenements. The ladder's bottom rung hung just out of reach of those at street level. I know the purpose of the fire escape is to get people down to street level, not lift them up from it, but all the same, that out-of-reach ladder gripped me. In my mind's eye, I saw a crowd of men, women, and children reaching for that ladder just beyond their grasp, desperate to escape the torment of the streets and the power of addiction.

My hope is that this book will help us get the escape ladder down to street level. My prayer is that it will help us bring hope to the hopeless, healing to the hurting, and wholeness to the broken.

This book isn't just about the places or the people that make the front pages. It's a book for London's suburbs, Latin America's megacities, West Africa's villages, and China's skyscrapers. It's a book for the communities where you and I work, rest, and play. It's a book not just for those dealing with substance abuse and addiction. It's a book for those ensnared by gambling addictions, porn dependencies, workaholism, out-of-control gaming habits, and technology-use disorders. This is a book about how slaves to addiction can experience freedom as children of the living God and family in the community of God—wherever they are, whatever it is that has enslaved them.

RAISED IN REHAB

I did my first night in rehab at five years of age. I didn't leave until I was 18. I was raised in rehab. It was the 1980s and the staff of Yeldall Manor, a residential rehab center in the southeast of England, mostly lived on-site with their families to create a sense of community for the men who joined the year-long program. In my family's case, that meant taking up residence in a small apartment on the first floor, right above the oak-paneled dining and games rooms. Yeldall Manor is no Downton Abbey, but nor would it be out of place in a BBC period drama. Its mock-Tudor architecture is set amid thirty-eight beautiful acres of park and woodland.

We ate our lunch and dinner together each day—staff, residents, and visitors. I'd eat quickly, and as soon as I could, I'd slip away to the pool table in hopes of a game with one of the residents or out onto the front lawn to play soccer or cricket. I'd roam the grounds for hours during school vacations, sometimes alone, sometimes with friends. We'd climb trees, build forts, play football, and ride bikes. Whenever I could, I'd help the guys with their work on the estate. When my parents went out, one of the more senior residents would come and watch us, entrusted with the care of my two brothers and me.

It was not an orthodox childhood, but I wouldn't trade it for the world. Naturally shy, I was sometimes ill at ease in a busy rehab, but I never felt unsafe. There was a real sense of security that came from being part of such a community, and as I grew older, I enjoyed building friendships with a diverse cast of characters you'd be hard-pressed to dream up.

Raised in such an environment, even as a kid, I was profoundly aware of the power of addiction. I knew it did great harm and caused great suffering. I knew that staying clean and sober was exceedingly difficult for the guys I shared my home with. What was going on in that place, in those men, was something deep and painful and precarious. On completing the program, some guys chose to stay around, so you knew whether they were doing well or not. Others moved away but would keep in touch, sometimes dropping in with wives and kids in tow or showing off a new car, undeniably enjoying life in recovery. Others would relapse. Some, of course, would lose their lives to addiction. Others would return to do the program for a second or third time. Occasionally, ex-residents would turn up unannounced, hurting and intoxicated.

I drink socially and have felt alcohol's subtle call toward a more "committed" relationship. As a young adult, I struggled to resist the pull of pornography. Today, I often wonder whether my smartphone serves me or I serve it. I don't, however, write as someone who has significant personal experience of addiction or recovery. If I set myself up as a recovery mentor, I certainly wouldn't pass muster with comedian and recovery champion Russell Brand, who said, "I wouldn't trust a Sherpa who at the foothills of Everest said, 'well, I've never been up before, but I've a hunch we'll be alright.'"[5] I take Brand's point. Those in early recovery benefit tremendously from having mentors who have "been there." However, after over a decade spent working in the addiction-treatment field, I've seen too much of the powerful role played by mentors, clinicians, therapists, pastors, and friends who are not in recovery to want to write them off entirely. Recovery happens in community, and the best communities are diverse.

Recovery happens in community, and the best communities are diverse.

Anyway, this isn't primarily a book for those who themselves are seeking freedom from addiction. It's not a self-help book. This is a book for the rest of us. Specifically, I've written with two groups of readers in mind. First, the church—its leaders, members, and educators. In a world that feels designed to lure us into addictive thinking and behaviors, this book is about how we should be the church together: *for, amongst,* and *as* people who are at risk of addiction, in active addiction, and in recovery from addiction. Second, the family and friends of those caught in the grip of addiction. This book is crafted in the belief that if we understand addiction and recovery better, we will be able to help one another more effectively.

PART ONE

THE AGE
OF
ADDICTION

ONE IN FIVE

THUNDERING HERD

I n a quiet corner of Spring Hill Cemetery, occupying an elevated position in the center of Huntington, West Virginia, an understated granite cenotaph pays silent tribute to the seventy-five men and women who perished in one of America's deadliest aviation disasters. Southern Airways flight 932 took to the air in Kinston, North Carolina, at 6:38 p.m. on Saturday, November 14, 1970. Marshall University's resurgent football team, the Thundering Herd, its coaching staff, and boosters were on board, heading home disappointed by a 17–14 loss to the East Carolina Pirates. It was the team's first flight of the year. Flight 932 would never reach its destination. Visibility was poor that night, with air-traffic control warning of rain, fog, smoke, and a "ragged ceiling" of clouds over Huntington's Tri-State Airport. The descending DC-9 clipped trees on a hillside west of the airport and crashed nose-first into a gully just over half a mile from the runway. Crash investigators would later describe the accident as "nonsurvivable."[1]

The devastating events of that night, powerfully depicted in the 2006 film *We Are Marshall*, profoundly shaped the people of Huntington. Indeed, as I talk to Steve Williams, mayor of Huntington, I notice a large portrait of that 1970 Thundering Herd team hanging behind his desk in his city hall office. A former member of the Marshall football team, Steve tells me why it occupies a place of pride and distinction in his office. "I have the portrait up here to let people know—if you want to understand the city, understand what happened there. This defines our city. We've been taken to our knees before, and we had the strength to stand up."[2]

This is my first time in Appalachia. As I explore Huntington, a small city of forty-five thousand people and three hundred-plus churches that hugs the south bank of the Ohio River, I feel far from metropolitan America and what I've experienced in places like New York, Miami, Las Vegas, San Francisco—and even further from the madness of LA's Skid Row. And yet, in the awkward gait and gray faces of some who walk these streets, there's a "tell," a sign that below the surface, Huntington is a small community wrestling with what we once thought of as a big-city problem: drug addiction. Specifically, an addiction epidemic centered on prescription painkillers, heroin, and a potent synthetic opioid called fentanyl.

In the days after August 15, 2016, global media outlets christened Huntington the "epicenter" of the US opioid crisis after twenty-eight people overdosed, two of them fatally, in the space of just five hours.[3] The following year, there were 1,831 overdoses, and 132 overdose deaths in Huntington and surrounding Cabell County.[4] Without naloxone, a drug that counters the effects of an overdose, hundreds more would have perished. To put it another way, in 2017 Huntington lost almost twice as many of its citizens to overdoses as it did to the 1970 Marshall air disaster.

Just a few short steps from the Marshall Memorial, the headstones of overdose victims stand tall among the many hundreds that fill the green lawns of Spring Hill Cemetery. It's hard to avoid drawing comparisons between the two tragedies. Both brought Huntington to international attention. Both have shaped the identity of the community. The first, abrupt and dramatic, afflicted the city's young heroes and became a source of strength and inspiration. The second unfolds slowly in dark rooms, riverside tents, hospitals, and courtrooms. Its victims are "junkies," men, women, and young people who fund their addictions through crime and prostitution.

DEATH GRIP

Huntington is just one of countless US communities—urban, suburban, rural—that find themselves in the relentless death grip of opioid addiction. Huntington's experience may be extreme, but it's not exceptional. Half of all Americans report knowing someone who has struggled with opioid addiction. Not an addiction in general—not even a drug addiction specifically. Half of Americans know someone who has struggled with *opioid* addiction.[5]

> Drug overdoses are the leading cause of death among Americans under fifty.

Data from the Centers for Disease Control and Prevention (CDC) reveals that drug overdoses in the United States surpassed a hundred thousand per year for the first time during the twelve months leading to April 2021.[6] These figures represent a 28.5 percent increase over the previous year, a jump explained by the rise in the use of fentanyl—a powerful synthetic opioid used to heighten the effects of heroin and cocaine, with or without the user's knowledge—as well as the impact of the COVID-19 pandemic.[7] Drug overdoses are the leading cause of death among Americans under fifty.[8] Across the whole population, they kill twice as many people as car accidents and gun violence combined.[9] A 2017 report by the news service

STAT, built on interviews with leading public health experts across ten universities, argues that between 2017 and 2027, opioids will claim close to half a million American lives.[10] The total number of American military personnel lost to armed conflict since the end of World War II, more than seventy-five years ago, stands at less than a third of that figure (152,883).[11]

It wasn't always this way. Drug overdoses on this scale are a relatively new public health issue. "The year 1979 was a turning point for the world's wealthiest nation," writes Timothy McMahan King in *Addiction Nation*. "That year marked the beginning of the exponential growth of drug overdoses in America. Out of every 100,000 people, 1.13 people died from an accidental drug overdose; in 2016 that number hit 16.96. Every nine years since [1979], drug overdose deaths have doubled, claiming a total of 599,255 lives . . ."[12]

The opioid crisis has grabbed the headlines and occupied our attention in recent years. However, opioids constitute just one part of a national substance-addiction epidemic that includes a range of other drugs and, of course, alcohol.

According to the National Survey on Drug Use and Health, in 2020, 40.3 million people aged twelve or older had a substance use disorder (SUD) in the past year.[13] Of these, 28.3 million had alcohol use disorder, 18.4 million had an illicit drug use disorder, and 6.5 million had both alcohol use disorder and an illicit drug use disorder. Today, the number of Americans addicted to drugs and/or alcohol exceeds the population of California.

Globally, best estimates suggest that about 1.4 percent have an alcohol use disorder,[14] while just under 1 percent have some form of illicit drug dependency.[15] That's 2 percent of the world's population addicted to alcohol and/or drugs.[16] And the number is rising. An international team of experts analyzed trends in alcohol intake in 189 countries. Their research, published in *The Lancet* in 2019, revealed that while alcohol consumption in high-income countries is stable or dropping, there has been a massive rise in low- and middle-income countries like India, China, and Vietnam. By 2030, it is projected that roughly half of all adults will drink alcohol, and 23 percent of the world population will binge-drink at least once a month.[17]

OBJECTS OF ADDICTION

A tremendous variety of substances enslave us. Methamphetamine addiction—use of which continues to rise across the US[18]—is also on the rise globally. In Southeast Asia, meth is the primary drug of concern in treatment.[19] In Bolivia, where I lived and worked for much of the past fifteen years, and in the other cocaine-producing countries of Latin America, coca paste—an intermediate product of the process of cocaine—is favored by street addicts, who smoke it with tobacco or cannabis. In the UK, Spice, a "synthetic marijuana" manufactured mainly in China and one of a vast number of new psychoactive substances (NPS) to hit the market in the last ten to fifteen years, has become a drug of choice in prisons. Studies suggest that 60 to 90 percent of the British prison population have used Spice while inside.[20] It's cheap, easy to smuggle, and hard to beat if you're killing time. "It just knocks you out cold," writes Mike Power in *The Guardian*. "And that's the point: users want total shutdown. . . . A few tokes and it's game over for six hours."[21] Across Africa, a crisis is unfolding with the prescription opioid Tramadol. In an article for *The Independent*, Laura Salm-Reifferscheidt writes, "Refugees in northern Nigeria . . . use Tramadol to deal with post-traumatic stress. In Gabon, it has infiltrated schools under the name Kobolo, leading to kids having seizures in class, while in Ghana, the 'Tramadol dance' is trending, basing its zombie-like moves on the way people behave when they're high on the painkiller. . . . Among the ranks of Boko Haram and Isis, Tramadol tablets are taken by fighters, leading them to be dubbed 'jihadist pills.'"[22]

In the middle of all this, it would be easy to overlook nicotine addiction. The World Health Organization estimates that smoking claims eight million lives every year, meaning one in seven global deaths are the result of tobacco (direct smoking and secondhand smoke). In several countries, including China and Denmark, more than 20 percent of deaths result from smoking. Tragically, as measures

As substance addictions rise, so does a second category of habits: behavioral addictions.

to reduce smoking in developed countries have proven effective, tobacco companies have shifted their marketing to low- and middle-income countries, with experts predicting that during the twenty-first century, a billion people could die as a result of tobacco addictions—ten times as many as died in the twentieth century.[23]

As substance addictions rise, so does a second category of habits: behavioral, or process, addictions. Activities widely considered to have addictive potential include gambling, work, exercise, pornography, sex, food, gaming, shopping, and the internet in a multitude of forms. Indeed, in the form of the globally ubiquitous smartphone, we are now physically connected—twenty-four seven in many cases—to the suppliers of the objects of addiction. In some cases, it may take a few minutes for the dealer to deliver, but likely no longer than your local pizza delivery service. In others, the product is just a click or two away, often—as in the case of online gambling platforms and clothing retailers—accompanied by powerful induce-ments designed to make it easier for you to dive in than to walk away.

An extensive study of behavioral addiction, published in 2011 and conducted by a team of researchers led by Professor Mark Griffiths of England's Nottingham Trent University, reviewed eighty-three research studies covering 1.5 million respondents from four continents. Its conclusion? Even back then, in the days before Apple's iPad and the launch of Instagram, 41 percent of us struggled with at least one behavioral addiction to the extent that it interfered with the performance of life roles (e.g., job, social activities, hobbies); impaired social relationships; led to criminal activity and legal problems; and spurred involvement in dangerous situations, physical injury and impairment, financial loss, or emotional trauma.[24]

We must not underestimate the extent of behavioral addictions nor their capacity to cause serious harm. Marc Lewis, a neuroscientist and recovering heroin addict, stresses the fact that "behavioral addictions assume the same characteristics, the same trajectory, and often the same outcomes as substance addictions . . . they too turn out to have serious consequences, including broken relationships, broken health, and sometimes death." What's more, Lewis explains, "the neural consequences of behavioral addictions indicate the same cellular mechanisms and the same biological alterations that underlie drug addiction."[25]

BEHIND EACH DIGIT

"Addiction today is epidemic and catastrophic," writes the neuro-scientist Judith Grisel. "Worldwide addiction may be the most formidable health problem, affecting about one in every five people over the age of fourteen. In purely financial terms, it costs more than five times as much as AIDS and twice as much as cancer. In the United States, this means that close to 10 percent of all healthcare expenditures go toward prevention, diagnosis, and treatment of people suffering from addictive diseases, and the statistics are similarly frightening in most other Western cultures."[26]

These are colossal numbers. And, behind each digit, you will find heartbreaking stories of personal suffering and sorrow. In *Beating the Dragon*, James McIntosh and Neil McKeganey draw on a series of intensive interviews with seventy recovering drug addicts from across Scotland to shed light on both addiction and recovery. Their reflections on addiction's impact on people's outlook, character, self-esteem, relationships, and health, as well as the way it led them into crime and other risky behaviors such as prostitution, make for sobering reading.

"My whole life," said Kenny, one of the interviewees, "was centered on drugs and any means to get them. My whole life revolved around drugs, drugs, drugs."[27] Maggie noted how addiction stole from her any sense of personal hygiene or self-care: "I used to be a clean person, my hair, my appearance. When I took drugs, that all went, and I used to have the same clothes on for weeks on end . . . stinking, not caring . . . as I say, these things don't matter when you've got a drug habit. They just go out the window."[28]

Steve described how years spent trying to fund his addiction turned him into someone no one could trust, a person he himself loathed. "I saw the ways I was going to get money to get drugs, and I didn't like it . . . shoplifting. I was breaking in, lots of sick things. I would rip off anybody. Someone would give me their trust, and that's me; I've ripped them off kind of thing. Like somebody would give me a loan of money, and I wouldn't pay them back. There were hundreds of these scams. Nobody trusted me anymore, know what I mean? I didn't trust myself anymore."[29]

Nancy detailed how addiction distorted her personality and, as a result, damaged her relationships. "I didn't recognize the person I was . . . I was just a nippy horrible person that fought with everybody; I didn't have a kind word for anybody. I spoke to people as if they were absolute dirt, and I wasn't really in a position to speak to anybody in that manner. I'd totally lost it. The person I'd turned into was just totally unbelievable."[30]

Bridie's addiction led her down a path she believed she would never go down and left her feeling worthless.

This friend of mine was in a massage parlor at the time . . . this was how she was feeding her habit. And all the things I said I would never ever do, I did it. I used to say I would never get to that stage. If I got as bad as that, I would stop. Then it's easier said than done. . . . So I went for an interview in a massage parlor and . . . I thought it was like a talking interview. But I later learned the interview wasn't. His very words were that he had to try me out to see if I was good enough. He paid me for it, and I walked out of there, and I felt so cheap and so dirty, but I was so tired of being arrested for shoplifting. I had nowhere else to turn, it was my only means of money, and basically the only things in mind was drugs, getting money for drugs. . . . My kind of day when I was working was work all night, sleep during the day, wake up about five, take my drugs, and out again to sell my body.[31]

Addiction's toll on Mary's physical health was the thing that ultimately prompted her to go after recovery seriously. "When I really decided I wanted to clean up, my health was zilch. I was covered in abscesses from head to toe, everywhere. I was only six stone [84 lb.], nobody would talk to me, nobody liked me, I didn't like myself. . . . So it came to the crunch when I decided to clean up, 'right Mary, you're either going to die young or you're going to clean up; what are you going to do?' And that's when I decided it's time to clean up."[32]

After a fourteen-year drug habit, Dorothy's recovery began with a similar reckoning with the damage drugs were doing to her. "I couldn't take it anymore. Mentally, physically, and spiritually I was broke. I was wasted. I was killing myself, slowly committing suicide. . . . I was going in and out of places, hospitals, and jails and institutions, and all that stuff. My brain and my body were so tired of it all. I'd had enough."[33]

Gambling, sex, and porn addicts will tell similar stories of gradual mental, physical, and spiritual decay. So, too, will alcoholics. All addictions lead down this path to ruin. Shopaholics run up unmanageable debts, lose trust in relationships, and find their mental health compromised. Workaholics place intolerable strains on their minds, bodies, and families. Gaming addicts untether from educational opportunities, pull away from personal relationships, and neglect nutrition and physical health.

Alongside the direct harm addiction causes to adults and young people, it has a devastating impact on children, whose stories are less commonly told. For decades, Gallup has asked the general population: "Has drinking ever been a cause of trouble in your family?" In 1948, 15 percent of respondents replied yes. By the early 1970s, it had dropped slightly to 12 percent. Since then, the figure has been rising steadily, reaching 37 percent in 2019—the highest number ever recorded.[34] Today, close to nine million children (12 percent of American children) live with at least one parent who has a substance use disorder.[35] In the year 2000, parental use of drugs and/or alcohol contributed to 18.5 percent of child welfare agency decisions to remove children to out-of-home care. By 2018, this figure had more than doubled after two decades of steady growth, to 39 percent of cases.[36] Also in 2018, one in ten pregnant women disclosed that they were current alcohol users, and 5.4 percent disclosed that they were current users of illicit drugs. That same year, 11.6 percent of pregnant women stated that they were current tobacco users.[37] From 2000 to 2012, the number of infants treated for neonatal abstinence syndrome (opioid withdrawal symptoms) increased more than fivefold.[38]

The parents in McIntosh and McKeganey's group of Scottish addicts in recovery didn't pull their punches as they described the

"You're either going to die young or you're going to clean up."

impact of addiction on their children. "I really neglected the kids because of my drugs," said Frances. "They weren't properly fed, and their clothes, just generally neglected. And I didn't bother with what they were doing, who they were going about with, how they were getting on at school or anything. It was just drugs, drugs, drugs."[39]

Another mother, Kathleen, confessed that she continues to be haunted by her failure to protect her son from abuse due to her drug-taking. "My eldest son had bruises on the side of his face, and I think it was my partner that hit him, but I was too out of my face to notice. I just hold on to things like that, what could have happened and what has happened."[40]

Mark expressed the same sense of abiding guilt for the harm caused by the priority he gave to drug-taking over his children's well-being. "I still can't put into words to this day how I feel about it. . . . He was parked in the room when people wanted to inject. If he didn't stay in the room, he'd maybe walk in, and we'd be sitting with a needle in our arm. He's seen a lot of things he shouldn't have seen, and that's what I feel guilty about."[41]

360°

Addiction once ran through our lives in narrow channels. Today, having burst its banks, it swamps a vast floodplain. Addiction is now the experience of the many, not the few. To use Stanton Peele's phrase, addiction is the "thematic malady of our society."[42] By the millions, we live as slaves to the neurochemical forces unleashed by a range of psychoactive substances and behaviors. We live under the ruinous shadow of an addicted parent, child, or partner by the tens of millions. Collectively, we suffer from the pressure addiction places on our economy and our health, social care, and criminal justice systems.

Christians must be realistic. Addiction is not an "out there" issue. The floodwaters of addiction have broken through the doors of our churches. In 2018, Lifeway Research surveyed a thousand Protestant pastors to understand their congregations' experience of the opioid crisis. Two-thirds said a family member of someone in their congregation had been personally affected by opioid abuse. More than half had someone dealing with opioid addiction in their congregation.[43] According to Barna Group research, 12 percent of youth pastors and 5 percent of pastors say they are addicted to pornography,[44] while among the wider church population, 21 percent of men and 2 percent of women say they think they are addicted to porn.[45]

Where you are, the addiction problem may be less severe—or just less visible?—than it is in Huntington, on Skid Row, in the cells of Britain's prisons, and the tents of northern Nigeria's refugee camps. Nevertheless, addiction is increasingly hard to ignore. As God's people, we live as "foreigners and exiles" (1 Peter 2:11) in an *addicted* world. Addiction is a feature of our missional context, an aspect of our cultures that we need to recognize, interpret, and engage.

Addiction is a 360-degree issue. It's behind us, shaping our personal and collective stories. It's around us, shaping our communities and how our neighbors think, feel, and act. It's ahead of us; all the evidence indicates that addictions of all kinds are on the rise. How did we get here? What is it about our times, and those that have gone before, that has ushered in an age of addiction?

Chapter 2

WHEN SUPPLY MEETS DEMAND

XALISCO HEROIN

The team that tends the neat lawns of Spring Hill Cemetery knows better than to mow the grass around the distinctive table stone that marks the grave of Adam Johnson. "They know I want to be the one to take care of it," says Adam's father, Teddy.[1] An aspiring musician, radio broadcaster, and Marshall University freshman, Adam was twenty-two when a heroin overdose took his life one fall weekend in 2007. In the previous six-and-a-half years, Huntington had suffered just four fatal overdoses. That weekend, three men died: Patrick Byars, forty-two, a Papa John's employee; George Shore, fifty-four, an artist who made his living selling antiques; and Adam Johnson.[2] By the end of the year, another nine would overdose and die.[3]

Huntington's addiction crisis would only come to international attention in 2016. However, heroin's infiltration into the community started to register that weekend. It came, as it already had across much of the US, in the form of Mexican black tar heroin. In his superb 2015 book, *Dreamland*, journalist Sam Quinones narrates the story of that sticky black substance's journey from rural poppy farms on Mexico's Pacific coast to the San Fernando Valley of Los Angeles and across the western United States to places as diverse as Portland, Salt Lake City, Maui, Anchorage, Denver, and Oklahoma City. Black tar heroin was first unloaded on American soil in the 1980s. Still, it was only in the late 1990s that it would make its way across the Mississippi River to Columbus, Ohio, and, from there, into the cities, suburbs, and small towns of the eastern United States. Its journey into the bloodstream of America was predicated on two things: purity and price. It gained market share because it delivered more bang for the buck than South American white powder heroin, which historically had dominated east of the Mississippi.[4] Something else, however, also played a critical role in the success of black tar heroin: the innovative approach of its Mexican traffickers, who all hailed from Xalisco County, Nayarit, a rural Mexican backwater where opium poppies are grown and processed into heroin.

Heroin's journey into the bloodstream of America was predicated on purity and price.

The traffickers from Xalisco operate like a "fast-food franchise" or "a pizza delivery service," an informant tells Quinones. "Each heroin cell or franchise has an owner in Xalisco, Nayarit, who supplies the cell with heroin. The owner doesn't often come to the United States. He communicates only with the cell manager, who . . . runs the business for him. Beneath the cell manager is a telephone operator. . . . The operator stays in an apartment all day and takes calls. The calls come from addicts, ordering their dope. Under the operator are several drivers, paid a weekly wage and given housing and food. Their job is to drive the city with their mouths full of little uninflated balloons of black tar heroin, twenty-five or thirty at a time in one mouth. "They look like chipmunks. They have a bottle of water at the ready so if the police pull them over, they swig the water and swallow the balloons. The balloons remain intact in the body and are eliminated in the driver's waste. Apart from the balloons in their mouths, drivers keep another hundred hidden somewhere in the car."

The traffickers' Xalisco kinship helps ensure each cell operating on US soil does so according to a set of shared values. "The cells compete with each other, but competing drivers know each other from back home, so they're never violent. They never carry guns. They work hard at blending in. They don't party where they live. They drive sedans that are several years old. None of the workers use the drug. Drivers spend a few months in a city and then the bosses send them home or to a cell in another town. The cells switch cars about as often as they switch drivers. New drivers are coming up all the time, usually farm boys from Xalisco County."[5]

TASMANIAN OPIOIDS

To fully understand black tar heroin's success, you must look beyond the qualities of the product and the creativity of its vendors to another psychoactive import, this one entirely legal: the opioids from Johnson & Johnson's poppy production on the island state of Tasmania, Australia, imported to manufacture hydrocodone (Vicodin) and oxycodone (Percocet, OxyContin).[6] Mexican traffickers weren't the first to bring opioids to the masses; pharmaceutical companies got there before them, supplying the population via a vast network of misinformed and, in some cases, unscrupulous physicians. The market for black tar heroin existed at the scale it did because communities across the length and breadth of the United States had a preexisting opioid habit to feed.

It would be hard to overstate the impact of prescription opioid painkillers on the US population since the turn of the century—or the extent to which the ubiquity of opioid painkillers is a distinctly American phenomenon. Approximately 80 percent of the global opioid supply is consumed on US soil by a little over 4 percent of the world's population.[7] University of Chicago research published in 2018 revealed that one-third of Americans had been prescribed opioids in the previous two years.[8] Prescription opioids were involved in close to 18 percent of opioid overdose deaths in 2020.[9] Between 2007 and 2012, according to Congress's Energy and Commerce Committee, 780 million hydrocodone and oxycodone pills were shipped to West Virginia (population 1.8 million).[10] In one two-year period, close to nine million pills were legally distributed to one pharmacy in Kermit, West Virginia (population 406). Undoubtedly, these opioids were diverted to "pill mills," where prescriptions were sold in bulk for cash, entirely within the bounds of the law.

Black tar heroin didn't precipitate a rush of new opioid addictions. It simply provided addicts with a replacement drug at a time when the state-sponsored supply was running out. "The overuse of prescription opioids," write economists Anne Case and Angus Deaton, "triggered the secondary epidemic of illegal drugs when Purdue introduced an abuse-resistant form of OxyContin and as physicians became more aware of the dangers and held back, or at least reduced the growth of the legal supply. . . . By 2011 it was too late to put the genie back in the bottle. Illegal heroin, an almost perfect substitute for oxycodone, quickly picked up the slack; deaths from heroin replaced deaths from prescription drugs, and the total overdose deaths continued its climb. Drug dealers waited outside pain clinics for patients whose doctors had denied them refills. Some bought (diverted) OxyContin on the street until discovering that heroin was both cheaper and more potent."[11]

ADDICTION BY DESIGN

How did we find ourselves in an addiction pandemic? The tragic story of America's de facto legalization of opioids illustrates the critical role of the supply side in creating addictions. It's not the only thing that matters; far from it. However, the supply tap of psychoactive chemicals and activities—whether cheap booze, online games, pornography, illegal drugs, or narcotics prescribed by a physician—must be open for addiction to flourish.

In his 2019 book *The Age of Addiction*, historian David Courtwright explores the growth and diversification of addiction through the ages and argues that today we find ourselves not just in an age of addiction but an age of "addiction by design." Across an array of industries, both legal and illicit, we design and market products with the express purpose of generating excessive consumption—even addictions—by targeting the limbic system, the brain pathways responsible for feeling, learning, motivation, memory, and quick reaction. Courtwright calls this "limbic capitalism," describing it as the "evil twin" and "cancerous outgrowth" of productive capitalism.[12] Limbic capitalism is by no means a new phenomenon. "Though the internet supercharged limbic capitalism, it did not invent it," Courtwright explains. He goes on:

> In fact, no one invented it. It emerged from an ancient quest to discover, refine, and blend novel pleasures. New pleasures gave rise to new vices, new vices to new addictions—for some people, anyway. Addictive behavior was seldom majority behavior. But the *risk* of such behavior grew as entrepreneurs rationalized—that is, made more scientific and efficient—the trade in brain-rewarding commodities. . . . By the nineteenth century, entrepreneurs were doing more than simply selling whatever new pleasures chance discovery and expanded trade

made available. They had begun to engineer, produce, and market potentially addictive products in ways calculated to increase demand and maximize profit.[13]

Limbic capitalists invented the "happy hour" to get us drinking more and drinking more quickly. They ensure that windows and clocks—anything that might signal the passing of time—aren't found in casinos. In the US, they ensure that while 10 percent of people ages fifteen to twenty-four have tried a Juul e-cigarette, most are unaware they contain nicotine.[14] Across the developing world, in places like Peru and Indonesia, limbic capitalists market cigarettes to schoolchildren, giving away free cigarettes and selling single fruit-flavored cigarettes at stalls within meters of school gates.[15] Limbic capitalists adopt predatory gambling marketing tactics, such as live-action and micro-betting, that shorten the delay between bet and reward and increase the speed and frequency of gambling to promote online sports betting.[16]

A professor at New York University's Stern School of Business, Adam Alter's book on the roots of various forms of technology addiction comes to the subject from the perspective of a digital marketeer. *Irresistible* is as unsettling as it is fascinating, highlighting the extent to which those who design online products ensure they are replete with a heady cocktail of goals, feedback, progress, escalation, cliff-hangers, and social interactions that make for a genuinely addictive experience.[17] Alter writes, "Instagram, like so many other social media platforms, is bottomless. Facebook has an endless feed; Netflix automatically moves on to the next episode in a series; Tinder encourages users to keep swiping in search of a better option. Users benefit from these apps and websites, but also struggle to use them in moderation."[18]

OPERATION GOLDEN FLOW

"The use of heroin by American troops in Vietnam has reached epidemic proportions," reported the *New York Times* on May 16, 1971. "The epidemic is seen by many here as the Army's last great tragedy in Vietnam. 'Tens of thousands of soldiers are going back as walking time bombs,' said a military officer in the drug field. 'And the sad thing is that there is no real program underway, despite what my superiors say, to salvage these guys.'" Correspondent Alvin Shuster concluded his report by asking a perennial question: "Like a parent who has suddenly discovered that his son is a junkie, the United States command has reacted with confusion and uncertainty. Should the kid be punished and kicked out of the house? Or should he be encouraged to confess all and be helped to recover?"[19]

As the troop withdrawal drew closer, and smoking marijuana was stamped out (75 percent of military personnel smoked marijuana), the soldiers' use of heroin had surged.[20] In the early '70s, there were more heroin addicts enlisted in the ranks of the US Army than in the civilian population back home.[21] Ninety enlisted men died from heroin overdoses in 1970.[22] Politicians stateside became increasingly concerned US towns and cities would be overwhelmed by junky veterans. President Nixon declared heroin addiction the nation's leading public health concern and the military launched a program, nicknamed Operation Golden Flow, which compelled returning soldiers who had ever tested positive for opiates to detox to prove they were clean with a urine sample before they could return home.[23] Back in the US, these soldiers were followed-up by authorities anxious to do everything in their power to prevent the kind of opioid crisis we face today.

A study published in the *Archives of General Psychiatry* drew together data gathered by Operation Golden Flow in Vietnam and face-to-face interviews with a cohort of 898 soldiers who returned from Vietnam in September 1971.[24] The study showed that "before arrival, hard drug use was largely casual, and less than 1% had ever been addicted to narcotics." While deployed in Vietnam, "almost half of the general sample tried narcotics and 20% reported opiate addiction," yet on returning to the US, "usage and addiction essentially decreased to pre-Vietnam levels."[25]

All of this raises two questions: Why did heroin use among service personnel reach such levels during their deployments? And how were so many of them able to leave their addictions behind them in the jungles of Vietnam?

In *The Age of Addiction*, David Courtwright refers to what he calls the "five cylinders of the engine of the mass addiction": accessibility, affordability, advertising, anonymity, and anomie.[26] The term "anomie" was coined by sociologist Emile Durkheim to describe when a society has lost common values and "new values and meanings have not developed." This lack of shared societal values can often lead to "psychological states characterized by a sense of futility, lack of purpose, and emotional emptiness and despair."[27]

In Vietnam, American soldiers found the engine of addiction firing on all cylinders. Detached from family and broader community structures, deployed military personnel operate within a distinct subculture that provides a form of anonymity and anomie. In Vietnam, soldiers had ready access to cheap heroin and little else on which to spend their money. *Time* magazine reported that heroin was "as common as chewing gum"—an exaggeration but one that reinforces a truth.[28] Heroin was advertised and promoted to soldiers, as Adam Alter vividly describes:

> Teenage girls sold vials from roadside stands along the highway between Saigon and the Long Binh US army base. In Saigon, street merchants crammed sample vials into the pockets of passing GIs, hoping they would return later for a second dose.

The maids who cleaned the army barracks sold vials as they worked. In interviews, 85% of the returning GIs said they had been offered heroin. One soldier was offered heroin as he disembarked from the plane that brought him to Vietnam. The salesman, a heroin-addled soldier returning home from the war, asked only for a sample of urine so he could convince the US authorities that he was clean.[29]

But is this the whole story? Or was there something about deployment, the life of a soldier far from home, the nature of warfare itself, that coalesced to create a hunger for heroin? How did the soldiers explain their heroin use? According to Professor Lee Robins, lead author of that 1975 study, participants responded that they used heroin because "it was enjoyable and made life in the service bearable."[30] It met a need. It provided a way to escape the harsh realities of a tour of Vietnam. Heroin satisfied desires created—or at least heightened—by the experience of a violent war. Once home, those desires diminished. As Dan Baum put it, "Take a man out of a pestilential jungle where people he can't see are trying to kill him for reasons he doesn't understand, and—surprise!—his need to shoot smack goes away."[31]

> A robust and plentiful supply is a necessary condition for the development of addiction. It is not, however, a sufficient condition.

Without access to cheap heroin and the liberty to enjoy it, heroin use and addiction among military personnel in Vietnam would never have reached the levels they did. The supply side does not, however, tell the whole story. A robust and plentiful supply is a necessary condition for the development of addiction. It is not, however, a sufficient condition. The supply side alone fails to explain why some soldiers did precisely what they were expected to do, continuing to use heroin back in the US, not least to navigate the trials associated with returning from the frontlines, including post-traumatic stress disorder (PTSD). The rest of the answer—perhaps the lion's share—is found on the demand side.

CITY OF SOLUTIONS

I drove to Huntington via Route 23 from Columbus, Ohio. The highway follows the Scioto River valley to the city of Portsmouth, where it takes a left, clinging to the banks of the Ohio River, toward Huntington. This whole area has been ravaged by addiction. For years, Route 23 functioned as a route out of Huntington for those leaving behind a city in economic and social decline. Since the late '90s, it has served as the main artery along which drug traffickers pump heroin into West Virginia. One highway. Two entirely different forms of escape for those struggling to bear up under the heavy yoke of modern life.

Arriving in Huntington, I expect to find one of two things: a city on the ropes, anxious and unsure in the face of a severe public health crisis, or a city in denial, unwilling to face reality. I find neither. In conversation after conversation with civic, community, and church leaders, it becomes clear that the people of Huntington are facing their addiction crisis square on. "We became extremely transparent about the extent of the opioid epidemic in our town . . . we acknowledged the brutal facts of what our community was facing," wrote Mayor Steve Williams in his foreword to *The City of Solutions*, a guidebook published to resource other communities confronting their opioid demons. The city took "aggressive action that resulted in a decline in overdoses, an increase in referrals to treatment, and a reduction in drug-related crime."[32] Today, Huntington describes itself as the "epicenter of the solution"—a community whose example others in the US and internationally are seeking to emulate.[33]

What have Huntington's leaders done to justify this pivot in the narrative? The current drugs strategy was developed in the shadow of a 2015 Huntington Police Department campaign dubbed Operation River to Jail, which sought to deliver on an earlier mayoral promise to "rain Hades down" on those bringing drugs into Huntington.[34] The city threw vast law-enforcement resources at disrupting the flow of drugs into the community. It was a classic "war on drugs" response to increasing drug consumption—an attempt to tackle addiction by using force to cut off the drug supply. In this case, that meant the arrest of more than 200 mostly out-of-town traffickers in just three months.

What could make more sense? Shut down the dealers, and you remove their products from the streets. Simple. But it didn't work like that. It rarely does. By Mayor Williams's admission, despite his biblical threats and the city's best efforts, the impact of Operation River to Jail at street level was negligible. The arrests made no impact. The traffickers simply deployed new personnel to meet Huntington's undiminished demand for opioids.

According to *The City of Solutions*, "Soon after, the city recognized that you could hardly tell any work had been done and decided there needed to be a shift in focus from the supply of drugs to the demand for drugs."[35] In the wake of the abject failure of Operation River to Jail (and the failure of countless comparable operations elsewhere), Huntington's quest to tackle opioid addiction trained its sights on two targets: first, reducing the demand for drugs; and second, reducing the harm caused by drugs.

To strike these two targets—demand and harm reduction—the city launched a range of initiatives. Priority was given to data collection and research, opening a needle exchange, naloxone distribution, and enhancing educational services. A multidisciplinary Quick Response Team was established and tasked with contacting all overdose victims to discuss treatment options within seventy-two hours of the overdose. This team included a paramedic, a law-enforcement officer, a recovery coach, and a faith leader. Cabell Huntington Hospital opened a neonatal unit dedicated to caring for drug-exposed babies. A drug court began steering nonviolent offenders away from incarceration and toward treatment. Treatment services—both medication-assisted and abstinence-based—were expanded. Together, these measures resulted in a 40 percent reduction in the headline issue of opioid overdoses between 2017 and 2021, and with a third of overdose calls ending with clients seeking addiction treatment, a first step on the road to recovery.[36]

In Huntington, the focus has shifted to the demand side. The city's goal is to diminish the demand for drugs and the harm caused by them by adopting an approach that elevates treatment above punishment, prevention above policing, and compassion above condemnation.

RAT PARK

Rat Park is the name given to a series of studies conducted by psychologist Bruce Alexander and colleagues at Simon Fraser University, British Columbia, in the late 1970s, highlighting the role of social context in the development and maintenance of addictions. Rat Park was, in fact, a sequel. During the 1960s and '70s, a new device called a Skinner box allowed researchers to create conditions in which laboratory animals could self-administer drugs by pressing a simple lever. This led to hundreds of experiments designed to observe how different animal subjects would respond to the limitless availability of various substances. Together, they appeared to demonstrate that certain drugs—including heroin, cocaine, and amphetamines—contain powerful chemical "hooks" that, once tasted, mammals are powerless to resist.

Avram Goldstein, founder of the School of Pharmacology at Stanford University School of Medicine, summarized the findings in a paper published in 1979: "If a monkey is provided with a lever, which he can press to self-inject heroin, he establishes a regular pattern of heroin use—a true addiction—that takes priority over the normal activities of his life . . . I have to infer that if heroin were easily available to everyone, and if there were no social pressure of any kind to discourage heroin use, a very large number of people would become heroin addicts."[37]

So why did Bruce Alexander feel the need for a sequel? Because human experience suggests the relationship between the availability of drugs and the onset of addiction isn't quite so simple. History demonstrates that even when substances such as opium, alcohol, and marijuana are readily available, only a small percentage of those who try them become addicted. Moreover, many manage—sometimes for decades—to moderate their consumption such that they can be described as "users" rather than "addicts." Something beyond the chemical makeup of these substances is in play when addiction develops.

"Laboratory rats are gregarious, curious, active creatures," writes Alexander in his brilliant book *The Globalization of Addiction.* "Their ancestors, wild Norway rats, are intensely social and, despite generations of laboratory breeding, their albino descendants retain many of their social instincts. Therefore, it is conceivable that rats may self-administer powerful drugs simply as a response to stress when they are housed in isolated metal cages. . . . The results of self-injection experiments may show nothing more than that severely distressed animals, like severely distressed people, will seek pharmacological relief if they can find it."[38] Might it be that the Skinner box itself was as much a cause of the rats' addiction as the heroin it dispensed?

To test his hypothesis, Alexander and his team constructed a social space, Rat Park, in which to run a self-injection experiment alongside a standard Skinner box. In contrast to the Skinner box, which housed a solitary animal alongside an endless supply of dope, Rat Park was designed to be a "psychosocial paradise" for rodents.

It accommodated thirty to forty rats, male and female, in an enclosure two hundred times the size of a standard laboratory cage. The morphine supply was accessed via a short tunnel leading out of the residential area, which the rats could only access one at a time.[39] Alexander, sounding like an aspiring Realtor, described the space as "airy and spacious . . . with a peaceful, British Columbia forest painted on the plywood walls, and rat friendly empty tins, wood scraps, and other desiderata strewn about the floor."[40]

A series of experiments was conducted using Rat Park. In one, the rats in both groups were force-fed morphine for weeks before entering the enclosures to ensure they began the experiment physically dependent on opiates. In another, the solution was sweetened to make it immediately and physically appealing to the rats. The result was fascinating. "Rats living in Rat Park had little appetite for morphine compared with the rats housed in isolation . . . in some conditions, the rats in the cages consumed nearly twenty times as much morphine as those in Rat Park. Nothing that we tried instilled a strong appetite for morphine or produced anything that looked to us like addiction . . ."[41]

HIBERNATION

"They speak of my drinking, but never my thirst," observes an ancient Scottish proverb of unknown origin. The Rat Park experiments turned the tables to find answers on the demand side. Why are we so thirsty? Why are increasing numbers unable to control their use of drugs, drink, sex, social media, online games, and food? Why have "excessive appetites" become so common?[42]

Bruce Alexander's answer, directed to those seeking to understand their own addictions, is this: "Addiction is an adaptation. It's not you—it's the cage you live in."[43] If we are to make sense of our age of addiction and gain ground in the war on addiction, we must give ample attention to the sociocultural context and the "cage" we live in. It's not the whole story, but it is a central feature. To do so is not to disregard the power of the objects of addiction and the destructive influence of a wide-open supply tap. Nor is it to suggest that spiritual condition, personal choices, and physiological attributes, are immaterial. To do either would be to oversimplify. However, we must acknowledge the extent to which addictions grow best in conditions that, in their hostility to human flourishing, kindle the demand for addictive experiences.

Why are increasing numbers unable to control their use of drugs, drink, sex, social media, online games, and food?

In this context, Alexander likens addiction to hibernation. It's an instructive and compelling analogy. "Hibernation is a costly adaptive process. Hibernation protects animals from the harshness of winter or other environmental stringencies. . . . This protective retardation of function comes at the cost of weakening the hibernating creatures, taxing their physiological systems to the limit, and making them vulnerable to predators. . . . Addiction, like hibernation, occurs when an individual cannot meet the demands of the environment and survives by adopting a diminished mode of functioning until the opportunity for more complete activity reappears."[44]

The supply side and the presence of high volumes of opioids, both prescribed and illicit, is by no means the singular cause of the US opioid crisis. Nor can it be explained simply with reference to the individual consumer's physiology, psychology, formative experiences, or spiritual condition. To successfully prevent and treat addiction, we must understand and address the demand side, examining the sociocultural "soil" in which individual addictions take root and grow.

Beneath the surface, where powerful substances and compelling activities dominate our attention, our thirst for the objects of addiction is driven by powerful forces. The millennial gamer staring at her computer in suburban Berlin, the retired alcoholic propping up the bar in the highlands of Scotland, the child smoking a cigarette a few meters from the gate of his primary school in rural Indonesia. Each has been shaped, imperceptibly and profoundly, by their social context—by family, community, society, and culture. What, then, is it about our society and culture that leads so many to slide, with reluctant willingness, into a state of human hibernation? We turn next to that critical question as we explore the root causes of demand.

Chapter 3

DESPAIR & EMPTINESS

MILESTONES

The son of award-winning journalists, my friend Tom was adopted in Russia, spent his childhood in Johannesburg, and navigated adolescence in New York City. His parents' work, reporting on the final years of the Cold War, the dissolution of the USSR, the end of apartheid, and the election of Nelson Mandela, put Tom within touching distance of the people who make and write history. It was a privileged life marked by affluence and adventure.

"I had a great upbringing," Tom tells me. "I was able to travel the world as a child and had incredible experiences. South Africa was awesome. I always heard about my parents going on crazy assignments around South Africa, Somalia, Rwanda, etc. We went on safaris, flew around in bush planes, and met all kinds of people. I remember going to a church with my nanny and having a very tangible experience of feeling God's presence, which drew me to going back to churches throughout my life."

South Africa wasn't all good, however. There was underlying stress to the lifestyle and traumatic experiences that remain etched in Tom's mind. "I remember watching a classmate's grandfather being carjacked and stabbed in front of me in the parking lot of my school. I watched the whole thing from the other side of the fence by myself. I had a confusing sexual encounter in my school that left me ashamed and broken for many years afterward. I remember running off and getting lost in various places in Johannesburg where we lived."

There are milestones on every journey into addiction that mark a significant shift in the nature of the relationship between the addict and the object(s) of their addiction.

In 1997, after a difficult few years in the suburbs of New York and the breakdown of his parents' marriage, Tom was transplanted to a classic brownstone on the Upper West Side, just a block from Central Park. "It was completely different from South Africa and even the suburbs," Tom recalls. "I can still remember showing up in New York City and being amazed by it."

Among a new group of friends, drinking, sex, drugs, and the buzz of the Big Apple, Tom found something he'd been missing for as long as he could remember—a sense of identity, self-worth, and connection. "I felt totally invisible my whole childhood. Suddenly, everyone knew who I was. My parents are very impressive people. However, they were also very driven, focused, high-profile, and sometimes emotionally unavailable. My mom ran a high-profile nonprofit. My stepdad was the foreign editor of an international news agency. My dad was the executive editor of a national newspaper. My stepmom was a famous foreign correspondent. I came from my grandfather's legacy of being the CEO of a large multinational. I was always amazed and interested in their lives, but my life sort of felt like an extension of theirs. My identity did too. I have always felt a huge pressure to fill their shoes."

Through drinking, drugs, porn, and sex, Tom also discovered a means of dealing with the dark and heavy emotions that dominated his inner world. "The divorce really hurt me. I lost all trust in my parents. I was very outgoing, trusting, and adventurous as a kid, even in South Africa. I would steal the gate remote, leave the house with my dog, and explore. My parents' divorce was the big thing that blew my life apart. I became very dark and morbid. I was troubled and distracted."

There are milestones on every journey into addiction that mark a significant shift in the nature of the relationship between the addict and the object(s) of their addiction. A new school in the Bronx was one such milestone for Tom. "I went to the town of Riverdale for junior high. There was just a totally different culture in the Bronx. Things started taking a turn in seventh grade. Then, at fourteen, everything took off. I looked up to the older kids, especially my best friend's older brother and friends. They all drank a ton, were known for pranks, smoked lots of weed, and became our idols. I remember buying a bunch of Sapporo beers and trying to impress them. I found and snorted my friend's mom's medication, and I was hooked. I skipped the first day of ninth grade to smoke weed for the first time and fell in love with it. I completely changed."

Despite a range of interventions—one-to-one therapy, a wilderness treatment program, twelve-step meetings, a sober house, a therapeutic boarding school—and short periods of sobriety, Tom's overall direction in those years was downward and into the arms of addiction. "The whole scene stopped being a party. I started having horrific and traumatic experiences on drugs, especially psychedelics, and the psychosis would endure long after the drugs had worn off.

My mental health had descended to a dark place—violent images, shouting, talking to myself, commanding voices telling me to hurt people and myself, seeing demonic figures. I was extremely depressed and was contemplating suicide at times. What started as experimenting with drugs and sex had turned a dark corner. I wanted to stop, but I really could not. It left me all very broken and confused and ashamed. At this point, I was just using more drugs and alcohol to numb out the pain from the things I was doing while intoxicated."

LANDMARKS

"Opiate addiction," observes Ann Marlowe in *How to Stop Time*, "only became a social problem when it became a social solution: when it addressed widespread longings and needs."[1] A key insight that we'll return to throughout this book is that addictions begin as solutions to problems—solutions that ultimately evolve to do more harm than the problem they were employed to solve. Addictions develop as individuals discover the curative effects of substances and activities that help them survive "life." Precisely what the addictive experience delivers varies from person to person. We're all different. Perhaps, like Tom, it's a sense of identity and an escape from difficult emotions. Perhaps it's the muffling of feelings of depression and anxiety. Maybe it's the silencing of inner voices that accuse, belittle, and shame. It could be a distraction from boredom and disappointment—or something else entirely.

Tom's story illustrates both the personal and social nature of these problems. An addiction is a highly personal state. It relates to *my* trauma, *my* shame, *my* anxiety, *my* pain, and *my* actions. It's also thoroughly social. The issues that make us vulnerable to addiction develop in the context of family units (nuclear and extended), community, and the broader society and culture. Addiction, like hibernation, is an adaptation to a hostile habitat. In the case of addiction, the habitat in view is the individual's social environment. However, where hibernation is seasonal—just one stage in a healthy annual cycle—addiction is a downward spiral. As addictions advance, they damage whatever lies in their path, causing the habitat to deteriorate further. Marriages fall apart. Jobs are lost. Debts mount. Health deteriorates. Legal problems form. Isolation intensifies. As a result, the need for addiction's enslaving solutions intensifies, the downward spiral into shame and despair tightens, and the inner resources needed to fight back drain away.

So, what's wrong with our cage? What are these widespread longings and needs that make us vulnerable to addiction? Why do we find ourselves in the age of addiction? The answers to those questions are infinitely complex. To pretend otherwise, oversimplifying or overstating our diagnosis or cure, does us no favors. Our very best efforts will only go partway toward explaining how sociocultural context influences human behavior as perplexing as addiction. What follows is therefore intended to be neither exhaustive nor definitive. My aim is simply to train a searchlight on four key features of modern life that ferment our burgeoning addiction problem. Like landmarks in an unfamiliar city, I hope that they will give us points of reference as we navigate our way around the world of addiction and recovery and think about what it means to be salt and light in the age of addiction. The better we understand the underlying causes of addiction, the better we will be able to shape public policy, design prevention strategies, reach and help those who are struggling, and become communities whose life together with God—Father, Son, and Holy Spirit—fosters healing, wholeness, and hope.

DEATHS OF DESPAIR

The first feature of modern life that nourishes mass addiction—particularly in the post-industrial societies of western Europe and the

US—is a widespread sense of hope-lessness. Despair drives addiction. The future is a source of profound concern to great numbers of us. In this, Huntington's story, though extreme, is illustrative of broader societal realities.

The first feature of modern life that nourishes mass addiction is a widespread sense of hopelessness.

When prescription opioids and black tar heroin landed on Huntington's streets, what did they find? In essence, a city that offered its inhabitants no sense of possibility. Those with aspirations, aspired to leave. Those who stayed, stayed hopeless. Sam Quinones described it well:

> The town was founded as a western terminus for the Chesapeake and Ohio Railway. Railcars carried the coal the region mined to Huntington, where river barges shipped it to the rest of the country. The city is at the nexus of America's North and South—much like West Virginia itself. . . . West Virginia sent its raw materials elsewhere to be transformed into profitable, higher-value products. Parts of the South threw off this third-world model of economic development. West Virginia did not. Resource extraction mechanized and jobs left. Railroads declined and economic turbulence set in. . . . Poverty intensified. Marijuana became the state's number one crop. . . . Immigrants avoided West Virginia. Only one percent of the state's population is foreign-born, ranking it last in that category in the United States. West Virginians with aspirations streamed north, thinking always of returning. . . . Many of the families who remained lived on government assistance. Huntington's population fell from eighty-three thousand in 1960 to forty-nine thousand today. The three R's became "reading, writing, and Route 23" as people headed north on the famous highway to Columbus, Cleveland, or Detroit. In

2008, the city was selected as the fattest in America; it had, the Associated Press reported, more pizza places than the entire state of West Virginia had gyms and health spas. Through all this, what grew steadily in Huntington, besides the waistlines of its dwindling population, was drug use and fatalism.[2]

Of these three—obesity, drug use, and fatalism—which is the deadliest? In truth, the first two are products of the third: a growing sense, particularly hazardous among young people, that no matter what you do, the future is bleak.

In *Deaths of Despair and the Future of Capitalism*, Princeton economist Anne Case and Angus Deaton (a 2015 Nobel Prize winner in economics) paint a "portrait of the American dream in decline."[3] In 2017, 158,000 Americans died due to just three causes: suicide, overdoses, and alcoholic liver disease/cirrhosis. That's a death toll equivalent to a weekly 9/11, or three Boeing 737s dropping out of the sky every day of the year.[4] Such a massive loss of life, Case and Deaton argue, is the product of despair: "For the white working class, today's America has become a land of broken families and few prospects. As the college-educated become healthier and wealthier, adults without a degree are literally dying from pain and despair. . . . Capitalism, which over two centuries lifted countless people out of poverty, is now destroying the lives of blue-collar America."[5]

J. D. Vance's memoir, *Hillbilly Elegy*, expresses the sense of hopelessness experienced by many who grow up in blue-collar America.

> You see, I grew up poor, in the Rust Belt, in an Ohio steel
> town that has been hemorrhaging jobs and hope for as long as
> I can remember. I have, to put it mildly, a complex relationship
> with my parents, one of whom has struggled with addiction
> for nearly my entire life. My grandparents, neither of whom
> graduated from high school, raised me, and few members of

even my extended family attended college. The statistics tell you that kids like me face a grim future—that if they're lucky, they'll manage to avoid welfare; and if they're unlucky, they'll die of a heroin overdose, as happened to dozens in my small hometown just last year.[6]

Pain and despair are by no means, however, the exclusive preserve of those living on the front lines of American deindustrialization. When you get down to it, you'll find fundamentally hopeless people from the suburbs to the cities, and everywhere in between. Despair is no respecter of persons. For increasing numbers across the US and throughout the world, it takes true audacity to hope for a better life than the one your parents enjoyed. The evidence suggests that such dreams are the stuff of fantasy and fairy-tale. Along with the ever-increasing availability of mood-altering substances and activities, this fact has helped pull us into an addiction epidemic. Johann Hari put it this way: "Ordinary Americans are finding themselves flooded with stress and fear. . . . All those stressed-out moms hooked on Vicodin, and all those truck drivers hooked on OxyContin have been seeing their incomes shrink and their abilities to look after their families wither for years as their status and security in American society shrivel away . . ."[7]

INFINITE ABYSS

Blaise Pascal, the seventeenth-century French mathematician and theologian best known for the philosophical argument known as Pascal's Wager, speaks of the "infinite abyss" within each one of us.

What is it then that this desire and this inability proclaim to us, but that there was once in man a true happiness of which there now remain to him only the mark and empty trace, which he in vain tries to fill from all his surroundings, seeking from things absent the help he does not obtain in things present? But these are all inadequate, because the infinite abyss can only be filled by an infinite and immutable object, that is to say, only by God Himself. He only is our true good, and since we have forsaken Him, it is a strange thing that there is nothing in nature which has not been serviceable in taking His place."[8]

Pascal was right. Just ask anyone who has pursued money, sex, and drugs with the kind of focus and abandon that goes into an addiction. If twenty-first-century consumerism and an addiction epidemic teach us anything, it's that no created thing can fill the emptiness at humanity's core.

The second feature of modern life that nourishes mass addiction is a widespread sense of emptiness. This is nothing new. However, the contemporary drive to fill the void by consumption of all kinds, combined with the corrosive effects of mobility and individualism on the quality of our relationships, has magnified an essential element of the human condition.

Emptiness is a common motif in the stories recovering addicts tell about the genesis of their addictions. Brad puts it this way: "I started taking drink and drugs at 10 or 11 because I never felt right in my own skin. There was always something missing."[9] My friend Tony says, "Drugs, alcohol, and crime filled the void inside me. Filling this void became my obsession."[10] Ann Marlowe writes: "The biggest, darkest secret about heroin is that it isn't that wonderful: it's a substance some of us agree to pursue as though it were wonderful because it's easier to do that than to figure out what is worth pursuing. Heroin is a stand-in, a stopgap, a mask, for what we believe is missing."[11]

Bruce Alexander gives a central place to this widespread sense of emptiness and our drive to address it in his work on the causes of addiction. "Human beings only become addicted when they cannot find anything better to live for and when they desperately need to fill the emptiness that threatens to destroy them. . . . The need to fill an inner void is not limited to people who become drug addicts but afflicts the vast majority of people of the late modern era, to a greater or lesser degree."[12]

The more we consume to satisfy our hunger, the greater our sense of lack and emptiness.

What do we do to fill the void? In one way or another, we consume. The underlying philosophy is the same, whether we reach for a takeout menu, a weekend city break, a games console, a gym membership, a new bathroom, or a new sexual experience. We try to convince ourselves: the more I consume, the more satisfied I will feel. The better things I consume, the happier I will be. Increasingly, the case goes further. Consumer spending is so critical to the modern economy that we're told our consumption is vital, not just to personal well-being but to societal health.[13]

The tools we use to create a fleeting sense of contentment, satisfaction, and peace are the dollars, pounds, or euros in our bank accounts. Credit cards and PayPal accounts give us access to the material goods which, bizarrely, we believe can meet immaterial needs. We use price tags to measure their capacity to slake our emotional, psychological, and spiritual thirst. The more exclusive the holiday, the more, we believe, it will gratify our yearning for rest and refreshment. The more expensive the restaurant, the more likely we'll go to bed with a contented smile. The more valuable the phone, the more satisfied we'll be as we gaze at its beguiling screen. All of this is, of course, tragically misguided and does us more harm than good. The more we consume to satisfy our hunger, the greater our sense of lack and emptiness. The more we consume to meet our emotional needs, the more vulnerable we become to developing both major and mild addictions.

In *Chasing the Scream*, Johann Hari interviews Canadian addiction expert Gabor Maté, who highlights the link between consumerism and the addiction epidemic. Hari writes:

> At the same time that our bonds with one another have been withering, we are told—incessantly, all day, every day, by a vast advertising-shopping machine—to invest our hopes and dreams in a very different direction: buying and consuming objects. Gabor tells me: "The whole economy is based around appealing to and heightening every false need and desire, for the purpose of selling products. So, people are always trying to find satisfaction and fulfillment in products." This is a key reason why, he says, "we live in a highly addicted society." We have separated from one another and turned instead to things for happiness—but things can only ever offer us the thinnest of satisfactions.[14]

TWO PATHS

The year 1979, observes Timothy McMahan King, was a watershed in the American addiction story. Why? Because it marked the start of a period of exponential growth of drug overdoses.[15] That year, on Sunday, July 15, President Jimmy Carter made a televised address to the nation. It was to have been a speech exclusively concerned with energy policy and an economy in recession. However, as he and his team began to prepare, Carter started to ask questions that would result in an address that was genuinely prescient, and perhaps prophetic: "I began to ask myself the same question that I now know has been troubling many of you," he said. "Why have we not been able to get together as a nation to resolve our serious energy problem? It's clear that the true problems of our Nation are much deeper—deeper than gasoline lines or energy shortages, deeper even than inflation or recession."[16] Carter's desire to search the soul of America led to a hastily organized presidential retreat at Camp David, to which "people from almost every segment of our society—business and labor, teachers and preachers, governors, mayors, and private citizens"—were invited.

In the light of that retreat, Carter wrote the address to the nation that would become known as the "malaise speech," a composition that speaks to the very sociocultural conditions that constitute an incubator for mass addiction: hopelessness about the future, inner emptiness, rampant consumerism, and the fragmentation of families and communities. In it he said:

> We've always had a faith that the days of our children would
> be better than our own. Our people are losing that faith,
> not only in government itself but in the ability as citizens to
> serve as the ultimate rulers and shapers of our democracy. . . .
> Just as we are losing our confidence in the future, we are also
> beginning to close the door on our past. In a nation that was
> proud of hard work, strong families, close-knit communities,
> and our faith in God, too many of us now tend to worship
> self-indulgence and consumption. Human identity is no longer
> defined by what one does but by what one owns. But we've
> discovered that owning things and consuming things does not
> satisfy our longing for meaning. We've learned that piling up
> material goods cannot fill the emptiness of lives which have no
> confidence or purpose.[17]

Toward the end of his speech, before he turned to the more prosaic matter of energy and economic policy, Carter called on the American people to acknowledge a fork in the road and to choose their path forward carefully. "We are at a turning point in our history. There are two paths to choose. One is a path I've warned about tonight, the path that leads to fragmentation and self-interest. Down that road lies a mistaken idea of freedom, the right to grasp for ourselves some advantage over others. That path would be one of constant conflict between narrow interests ending in chaos and immobility. It is a certain route to failure. All the traditions of our past, all the lessons of our heritage, all the promises of our future point to another path, the path of common purpose and the restoration of American values. That path leads to true freedom for our nation and ourselves."

Ours is the age of addiction. How did we get here?

More than forty years from Carter's Camp David retreat and the televised address that followed, we are left with no doubt which of these paths was taken. The only question we now face is whether there is a will, and a way, to change course.

Ours is the age of addiction. How did we get here? To understand addiction and to successfully prevent and treat it, we must look beyond the powerful substances and stimulating activities that dominate the foreground. The supply side is just one element of the problem. The demand side is every bit as important.

Four features of modern life contribute to this demand, shaping us in ways that leave us vulnerable to the lure of the enslaving solution found in addictive experiences. We have explored the first two in this chapter: a pervasive sense of hopelessness, even despair, and a widespread sense of emptiness and dissatisfaction. We turn now to the next two: the degree to which adverse childhood experiences impact us as we move through adolescence into adulthood, and the extent to which we have come untethered from one another and a sense of belonging that is vital to health and well-being.

Chapter 4

ADVERSITY & DISCONNECTION

CANAL KIDS

In Santa Cruz de la Sierra, the tropical Bolivian city where our family has made its home for much of the past fifteen years, the stoplights at major intersections do much more than manage traffic flow. They play host to a hive of commerce, entertainment, and charity. Before your vehicle comes to a halt, men, women, and children—all there to make ends meet—swarm toward you. Vendors tout drinks, newspapers, fruit, desserts, electronic accessories, toilet paper, and more. Seasonal specials appear like clockwork: orchids on Mother's Day, roses for Valentine's, fireworks around New Year's, and flags for Independence Day. Kids dash about with soap and squeegees, eager to clean windshields. Dancers perform and musicians play. Now and again, circus performers appear juggling fire, swallowing swords, and walking makeshift tightropes. In the middle of all that, the poor and sick move about quietly searching for financial help.

As I sit at the lights, wondering how best to navigate the needs before me, I'm often struck by the social diversity of the communities that, every ninety seconds, gather and disperse at these stoplights. Where and when else does such a diverse collection of *cruceños* (residents of Santa Cruz) gather? For a few moments, those scraping together a living by selling are joined by old money and the new rich in their SUVs, workers packed inside buses, students on bicycles, tradespeople on motorcycles, and newly minted middle-class families in their small cars.

The wounded underclass of homeless addicts is there too. They're part of the swarm, washing windshields and begging, but mostly they're hidden from sight. Santa Cruz is crisscrossed by a network of open drainage canals built to prevent flash floods by carrying rainwater to the wide brown river that skirts the city's western edge on course to the Amazon. Where the open canals meet road intersections, they tunnel under the asphalt. In these tunnels, the city's street people establish camps where dozens of them eat, sleep, wash, and get high together, just a few feet below the bustling activity above.

The dark, dank conditions inside these camps are conducive to little more than decay, disease, and despair. They're dehumanizing, soul-destroying environments. Indeed, if you pass one spot regularly enough, you'll notice familiar faces deteriorate before your eyes—skin, hair, and eyes signaling that life is draining away. The canals are dangerous. Violence is both the *lingua franca* of conflict resolution within the community and the preferred tactic of the law-enforcement unit tasked with policing the homeless population. The rainy season's tropical downpours, which often arrive suddenly and at night, drive torrents of dirty water through the tunnels, trapping and drowning anyone too intoxicated to notice in time to escape.

A quarter of those living in the canals are children, and a third of those are under twelve. Many adults have been on the streets since they were children or adolescents.[1] As might be expected, the tight orbit of these communities rotates around drugs, substances that offer an all-encompassing escape, a gateway to hibernation. Three-fourths of Santa Cruz's street people admit to the authorities that they consume drugs. The kids prefer inhalants, adolescents choose marijuana, and the adults move between alcohol, marijuana, and coca paste (cocaine before it is purified and converted into cocaine or crack).[2]

> **What is it about the alternative that causes so many young people to descend into the darkness?**

What is it that pulls people into such squalor? What's the push? What is it about the alternative that causes so many young people to descend into the darkness? The stories of two friends—both graduates of the Novō Communities residential program in Santa Cruz—represent those I hear repeatedly.

"I'm twenty-five years old, the youngest of seven siblings," says Sergio. "My childhood was very hard. My father worked all day and was very hard on me. My mother only came to sleep at night. I was put into a children's home at six years old. At seven, I started with marijuana and cigarettes because I saw my brother who smoked, and when I was nine, I started drinking alcohol. In the street, everyone used drugs and alcohol, so I used myself so they wouldn't call me [horrible names]. I used to be respected. On the street, there were no rules, and I felt free. In the children's home, I felt like a slave."

Benigno has a similar story. "When I was a child, I was on my way to school, and one day, out of curiosity, I followed my friend, and he went online. I ended up addicted to the internet. I collected money to go to internet cafés and stopped going home at night. I slept at a petrol station and then when I was about seven years old, they sent me to a children's home. After six months, I left with a friend, but I didn't know Santa Cruz, and I got lost. Since then, I have lived on the streets. I would search for food to eat in the garbage, or people would give me leftovers. I also went to a dining room for street kids, where some of the kids introduced me to *clefa* [glue]. It made me feel drunk. I really liked it and couldn't stop. After *clefa*, I started using alcohol and marijuana."

ACEs

To make sense of today's addiction epidemic, we must shine our searchlight on the prevalence of adverse childhood experiences (ACEs). Adversity is the third feature of modern life that nourishes mass addiction.

Addiction expert Stanton Peele, writing in 1977, was among the first to give popular voice to the idea that addiction is not rooted wholly, or even primarily, in the objects of addiction but rather in the life experience of its subjects. "All data point to the fact that addiction is a lifestyle, a way of coping with the world and ourselves," Peele argued in *The Addiction Experience.* "Heroin and alcohol do have a powerful impact on both a person's body and feelings, but these effects do not in and of themselves cause addiction. The core of the addiction is how the person interprets and responds to the impact of the substance. This is determined by the individual's feelings about self and about life, as these are, in turn, determined by childhood experiences, personality, and current social setting."[3]

The most influential research into the impact of childhood adversity on adult health is the Adverse Childhood Experiences Study, conducted at Kaiser Permanente's San Diego Health Appraisal Clinic in association with the CDC.[4] From 1995 to 1997, a super-sized sample of seventeen thousand–plus ethnically diverse, middle-class adults, with an average age of fifty-seven, were surveyed about their childhood experiences and present-day health. The goal was to understand the long-term relationship between childhood experiences and adult physical and mental health, including addiction. At the time of the survey, the health status of the sample was representative of the general population.

A distinction was made between three categories of adverse childhood experiences in the questions posed to the participants: 1) Abuse (emotional, physical, and sexual); 2) Household Challenges (substance abuse, mental illness, domestic violence, parental divorce/separation, an incarcerated household member); and 3) Neglect (physical and emotional).[5]

The prevalence of these experiences in the childhoods of those surveyed—and, by extension, the childhoods of the general population—should give us pause. Nearly 25 percent of the women, and 16 percent of the men, had been sexually abused. Fully 28 percent had experienced physical abuse, defined as "often or very often" being pushed, grabbed, shoved, slapped, or "hit so hard that you had marks or were injured." Twenty-seven percent had lived with someone who was an alcoholic, "problem" drinker, or illicit-drug user. Finally, 23 percent had lived through the divorce or separation of their parents.[6]

Each participant in the study was given an ACE score of between 0 and 8, based on the number of *types* of ACEs experienced during childhood/adolescence. A striking correlation emerged when researchers analyzed the relationship between addiction and ACE score. Adults with ACE scores of 6 or more were three times more likely to smoke than those with no severe adverse childhood experiences. Adults with ACE scores of 4-plus were five times more likely to become an alcoholic than those spared severe adverse childhood experiences. Men with an ACE score of 4-plus were forty-six times more likely to become injection-drug users than those with no severe adverse childhood experiences.[7]

Dr. Vincent Felitti headed up the study and summarized its findings in relation to the origins of addiction:

The basic causes of addiction lie within us and the way
we treat each other, not in drug dealers or dangerous
chemicals. . . . Our findings indicate that the major factor
underlying addiction is adverse childhood experiences. . . .
Adverse childhood experiences are widespread and typically
unrecognized. These experiences produce neurodevelopmental
and emotional damage, and impair social and school
performance. By adolescence, children have sufficient skill
and independence to seek relief through a small number of
mechanisms, many of which have been in use since biblical
times: drinking alcohol, sexual promiscuity, smoking tobacco,
using psychoactive materials, and overeating.[8]

JORGE & TIM

The motifs of neglect, abuse, and household dysfunction feature
strongly in the childhood stories of the men who step through the
heavy oak doors of Yeldall Manor in search of healing, wholeness,
and hope. For many, Yeldall's treatment program represents a final
opportunity to get intensive addiction treatment. It's the last-chance
saloon, a place where they must tackle the past, engage the moment,
and prepare for the future if they are to find lasting freedom. To do
so they must be courageous, humble, and determined.

"I was born in Mozambique to a well-off family and had all
a boy could need," says Jorge. "But my dad worked away, and my
mum was out at bridge parties and so on. At four, I was sent away to
boarding school. I hated it and couldn't understand the separation
from my parents. From an early age, I felt different and alone. When
I was 14, I was kidnapped and held for ransom for three months
during which time I was abused. When I was released, there was no
help. I just went back to school and got on with life. That was it." It
was a decade later that Jorge started to use drugs seriously. "I was 24

70

when I got into drugs," he explains. "It took me to a place of despair. I felt lost and lonely. I was in a very dark place indeed."[9]

Mike's childhood story was less dramatic, but it left him similarly wounded. The youngest of three siblings, his life looked good from the outside, but things were far from okay behind closed doors. During frequent violent arguments between his parents, Mike would hide upstairs with his siblings, out of harm's way but fearful. Certain that he was the cause of their problems, Mike would sit in silence, alone at the top of the stairs, listening to their rows for proof that he was to blame. At seven, he started to be bullied at school, and his one happy place, a refuge from the volatility of home, was gone. Steeped in shame and brimming with anxiety, Mike was haunted long into adulthood by an unspoken question, "What's the matter with me?"

In alcohol, Mike found no satisfactory answer to that question, but he did find a way to muffle the inner voices that accused and belittled him. More than that, when he drank, he discovered self-assurance and inner peace. Alcohol carried Mike through his early teenage years, filling in for his absent and angry parents. It began with cider and cheap wine in the local park, a way to fit in with friends before youth club. Before long, girls even began asking him out! When Mike's mum left home, leaving him behind with his dad, things began to get more intense. Social drinking quickly evolved into serious alcohol addiction. "By the time I was 15," he says, "I knew I had an issue. I was starting to drink half a bottle of vodka a night, and that was my coping mechanism to try and deal with my life. I just didn't want to think about anything that was going to hurt me. I just wanted to escape from it."[10]

STEP INSIDE THE CIRCLE

"Is everyone ready to face their past with compassion?!" Shouting the question across the vast gravel exercise yard of a maximum-security prison is Fritzi Horstman, founder of the Compassion Prison Project. A petite blond in her fifties, Fritzi cuts an incongruous figure as she stands encircled by over two hundred inmates beneath the fierce Southern California sun. Facing her, the inmates wear identical sky-blue prison tunics and faces heavy with apprehension. In contrast, Fritzi wears a black T-shirt emblazoned with simple words of reassurance: "There is no shame."

She asks again, "Is everyone ready to face their past with compassion?!" This time, the inmates deliver their reply in unison, "Yes!"

It's February 2020, and Fritzi is leading the group in an exercise developed with their input, the Compassion Trauma Circle. Today's circle is being documented for a profoundly moving film, *Step Inside the Circle*.[11] A series of questions, built on the Adverse Childhood Experiences Study findings, follow Fritzi's initial invitation.

"While you were growing up, during your first eighteen years of life, if a parent or other adult in the household would often, or very often, swear at you, insult you, put you down, or humiliate you . . . step inside the circle." Most of the men step forward.

> **Almost to a man, you can see the boy beneath—still hurting, confused, longing for a father's love.**

"If a parent or other adult in the household often, or very often, pushed, grabbed, slapped, or threw something at you . . . step inside the circle." Again, most of the men step forward.

"If you often felt that no one in your family loved you, thought you were important, or special . . . step inside the circle." More step forward.

With each new question, hundreds of heavy boots stride forward; the men, wearing a variety of scarves, tattoos, and scars, move closer together, their faces a paradox of hardness and vulnerability. Almost to a man, you can see the boy beneath—still hurting, confused, longing for a father's love; still in need of acceptance, affirmation, encouragement, and protection.

Afterward, in a group setting indoors, the men share. "Our traumas kept us separated," one of them explains. "We were all on the circumference; we were all standing apart. But, once we began to acknowledge our traumas publicly, it bought us all closer together."

"I'm a traumatized child, raised by a traumatized child," says another. "My mother didn't want me. She hid her pregnancy, and she tried to flush me down the toilet. As I learned about these things, I always asked myself what was wrong with me."

WHY THE PAIN?

Gabor Maté was born in Nazi-occupied Budapest. His grandparents were killed at Auschwitz and his father spent the first fifteen months of Gabor's life in a forced-labor camp. Not knowing whether her husband was dead or alive, and reeling from her own trauma, Gabor's mother struggled to care for her newborn son, often leaving Gabor alone in his crib for hours at a time.[12] Reading *In the Realm of Hungry Ghosts*, it's clear that Maté's outlook has been profoundly shaped by his reflection on his childhood and his own experience of addictions, as well as twelve years of medical practice, serving in Vancouver's Downtown Eastside. What results is an approach to addiction and recovery centered on the issue of adverse childhood experiences. "Not all addictions are rooted in abuse or trauma," he writes, "but I do believe they can all be traced to painful experience. A hurt is at the center of all addictive behaviors. It is present in the gambler, the internet addict, the compulsive shopper, and the workaholic. The wound may not be as deep and the ache not as excruciating, and it may even be entirely hidden—but it's there."[13]

Gabor argues that if we want to help those in addiction effectively, our question should not be, "Why the addiction?" Instead, we need to ask, "Why the pain?"[14]

RELATIONSHIPS, RELATIONSHIPS, RELATIONSHIPS

The US cigarette company Philip Morris International is one of the giants of limbic capitalism. Second only to the China National Tobacco Corporation, which sells 99 percent of its cigarettes within China,[15] Philip Morris products account for 14 percent of a global cigarette market whose growth is found exclusively in low- to middle-income countries, driven in no small measure by clever marketing directed at children.[16] A staggering 8.2 million people die prematurely each year due to tobacco use; seven million are direct tobacco users; and 1.2 million die from exposure to secondhand smoke—almost as many as are killed in road traffic accidents worldwide.[17] Given Philip Morris's starring role in the global addiction story, there is some irony in the fact that one of the most important studies of human physical and mental health owes its existence to their patronage.

The Harvard Study of Adult Development was born in 1938, in the gloom of the Great Depression. Today, more than eight decades later, it's alive and kicking and focused on providing answers to one far-from-simple question: What makes a good life? The study was conceived in the mind of Dr. Arlie Bock, a Harvard physician, who believed that "medical research paid too much attention to sick people; that dividing the body up into symptoms and diseases—and viewing it through the lenses of a hundred micro-specialties—could never shed light on the urgent question of how, on the whole, to live well."[18] For the study, 268 Harvard sophomores (all men) were recruited so that a multidisciplinary team of specialists could study them "from every conceivable angle and with every available scientific tool."[19] Moles were measured, scrotums analyzed, and handwriting samples taken. Family histories—medical and social—were scrutinized.

The study started well but by the mid-1950s it was "on life support," serviced by a lone psychologist, Chuck Heath, who had access to scant resources. It was then that Philip Morris, along with the Rockefeller Foundation, stepped in to pump oxygen into the lungs of the study. In return, Harvard agreed to include questions about the smoking habits and cigarette-brand preferences of the group. One survey included the question, "If you never smoked, why didn't you?"[20]

The study got its new lease on life in the nick of time. The original participants were now middle-aged and as their physical and mental health began to diverge, the study began to yield significant insights. To broaden its scope, the study was extended to include a group of 456 disadvantaged young people who had grown up in Boston's inner-city neighborhoods in the early 1940s. The children of the participants were also recruited to join the study: 1,300 of them, now in their fifties and sixties. Eventually, the wives of the Harvard alumni were added.[21] Today, the Harvard Study of Adult Development utilizes MRIs, DNA testing, and the latest psychological assessment tools to deepen our understanding of what makes a life, measured over its entirety, healthy and happy.

In George Vaillant, who led the study for three decades from 1967, the study found its "storyteller"—a baton now carried forward by its current director, Harvard psychiatrist Robert Waldinger.[22] Reflecting on the study as a whole, both men share a conclusion that could scarcely have been predicted back in 1938, when Dr. Bock and his team began following the original Harvard cohort, including one with the initials JFK.[23]

Vaillant is unequivocal in his interpretation of the study's findings: "When the study began, nobody cared about empathy or attachment. But the key to healthy aging is relationships, relationships,

relationships."[24] Indeed, the study demonstrates that, among both the Harvard and inner-city participants, strong relationships are a better predictor of physical health, longevity, and happiness than class, wealth, fame, IQ, or genetics. "The really surprising finding," says Waldinger, "is that our relationships and how happy we are in our relationships has a powerful influence on our health. . . . The people who were the most satisfied in their relationships at age 50 were the healthiest at age 80. Strong relationships help to delay mental and physical decline. Taking care of your body is important, but tending to your relationships is a form of self-care too. That, I think, is the revelation."[25]

LONELINESS KILLS

To understand the age of addiction, the fourth feature of modern life onto which we must cast our searchlight is a widespread and growing sense of social disconnection. Addiction is on the rise—as are the related disorders of depression and anxiety—in no small part because fewer and fewer of us have the kinds of close, enduring relationships needed for physical, emotional, and spiritual well-being. Instead, we're isolated, bereft of life-giving, one-to-one relationships and a sense of belonging and community. We live as if we were "an island entire of itself."[26] As a result, we suffer profoundly.

Our need for one another is elemental. God is a social being— three persons in a loving relationship—and, as bearers of His image, we are fundamentally relational beings for whom "it is not good" to be alone (Gen. 2:18). And yet, *alone* is precisely the state in which we find ourselves, as advances in transport and communication made possible by the Industrial Revolution, and now the internet revolution, have pulled us apart, not together. And it is not good.

"Loneliness kills," Robert Waldinger asserts. "It's as powerful as smoking or alcoholism."[27] Additionally, severe loneliness—and the milder form of the condition yielded by the distant, superficial, and transitory nature of many of today's relationships—is a crucial driver of addiction and a leading cause of relapse among those in recovery. "The connection between loneliness and alcohol addiction is illustrated almost ad nauseam in the 'Personal Testimonies' of AA's Big Book," writes Kent Dunnington in *Addiction and Virtue*. "It is by far the most common theme."[28]

> **Our need for one another is elemental.**

My friend Keith's story—a childhood of material well-being that failed to compensate for a deficit of parental love and attention—is tragically unremarkable. "I was brought up in a nice middle-class area, reasonably well-off, quite a good upbringing," he says. "But I was never shown much love or affection. My parents were always working, arguing, and drinking in the evenings. I was just lost. I didn't feel like anyone loved me. I didn't feel like I belonged anywhere."[29]

As she often does, Ann Marlowe describes the experience of drug use in terms that help the uninitiated to make sense of the experience, highlighting its capacity to neutralize feelings of loneliness and psychological homelessness. "Like travel to faraway places, heroin served as a way of rendering my solitude beside the point. Doing it alone added no opprobrium; that was the least of my worries. And it made sense; the drug was a companion. . . . Being high allowed me to enjoy being alone without loneliness. . . . When I stopped getting high, what bothered me most was my relapse into loneliness, or into the awareness of it. . . . Dope made it easier for me to stay at home; dope was a home, a psychic space that filled the essential functions of the physical construct, providing a predictable comfort and security."[30]

FLYING SOLO

In his influential book *The Globalization of Addiction*, Bruce Alexander (of Rat Park fame) contrasts two states—psychosocial integration and psychosocial dislocation—representing opposite ends of a continuum of personal well-being. On the one end, *psychosocial integration* refers to a state of deep interdependence between the individual and the community around them that develops over the course of their life. "Psychosocial integration," writes Alexander, "reconciles people's vital needs for social belonging with their equally vital needs for individual autonomy and achievement. Psychosocial integration is as much an inward experience of identity and meaning as a set of outward social relationships."[31] On the opposite end of the spectrum, *psychosocial dislocation* refers to a state of fundamental disconnection between the individual and society. To be psychosocially dislocated is to be detached, independent, flying solo without the deep friendships, sense of belonging, shared identity, and sense of meaning that come from being part of a healthy community.

The forces that create states of psychosocial dislocation are legion. It's a state that a handful of people choose, but most have foisted upon them. Perhaps a natural disaster forces a community to disperse, or the community rejects an individual due to criminal behavior. "It can be inflicted with the best of intentions," writes Bruce Alexander, "by inculcating an unrealistic sense of superiority that makes a child insufferable to others or by flooding a local society with cheap manufactured products that destroy its economic basis. It can be chosen voluntarily if a person is drawn from social life into the single-minded pursuit of wealth in a 'gold rush' or a 'window of opportunity.'"[32]

Alexander argues that where we find abundant addiction, we will find a scarcity of psychosocial integration. Throughout history, addiction has followed in the wake of the kinds of social change that prompt widespread social breakdown. Johann Hari summarizes the historical evidence Alexander marshals to make his case. "The native peoples of North America were stripped of their land and their culture—and collapsed into mass alcoholism. . . . The English poor were driven from the land into scary, scattered cities in the eighteenth century—and glugged their way into the Gin Craze. The American inner cities were stripped of their factory jobs and the communities surrounding them in the 1970s and 1980s—and a crack pipe was waiting at the end of the shut-down assembly line. The American rural heartlands saw their markets and subsidies wither in the 1980s and 1990s—and embarked on a meth binge."[33]

Today, as we enter the third decade of the twenty-first century, Alexander argues that psychosocial dislocation is no longer an aberration. Increasingly, it's the normal state of those who live in modern and modernizing societies. Modernization, explains sociologist Steve Bruce, is "a multi-faceted notion, which encompasses the industrialization of work; the shift from villages to towns and cities; the replacement of the small community by the society; the rise of individualism; the rise of egalitarianism; and the rationalization both of thought and social organization."[34] The negative impact of modernization—and, of course, there are a great many positives—is turbocharged by free-market capitalism that rewards individualism, competition, and constant change.[35]

The age of addiction is the product of an age of psychosocial dislocation. "Today's flood of addiction," Bruce Alexander argues, results because "our hyper-individualistic, frantic, crisis-ridden society makes most people feel socially or culturally isolated. Chronic isolation causes people to look for relief. They find temporary relief in addiction . . . because it allows them to escape their feelings, to deaden their senses—and to experience an addictive lifestyle as a substitute for a full life."[36]

RETROGRADE METAMORPHOSIS

Judith Grisel, whose story of addiction and recovery underpins her book on the neuroscience and experience of addiction, *Never Enough*, is quite clear that addiction provides real-world solutions to the inner-world problems these features of modern life produce. Tragically, as addicts of all stripes will readily testify, addiction—a chrysalis that plays host to a retrograde metamorphosis—all too quickly transforms into a far more significant problem than the one that, for a time, it solved. "In the end," she writes, "the very effect I loved so much about alcohol—its ability to mute existential fears— utterly betrayed me. It didn't take all that long before the drug's most reliable effect was to ensure the alienation, despair, and emptiness that I sought to medicate. . . . Rather than provide a solution to my problems with living, [alcohol and drugs] had chipped away at every prospect until only the barest shred of life remained. I'd sought wellness and became sick; fun, but lived in a constant state of anxious dread; freedom, and was enslaved. In just ten years, my sources for solace had totally betrayed me, carving out a canyon deep and unlivable."[37]

Comedian and recovery activist Russell Brand delivers a similar diagnosis. "We adapt to the misery of an unloving home, of unfulfilling work. Of empty friendships and lacquered alienation. . . . The instinct that drives the compulsion is universal. It is an attempt to solve the problem of disconnection, alienation, and tepid despair because the problem is ultimately 'being human' in an environment that is curiously ill-equipped to deal with the challenges that entails."[38]

What is it about the modern world that has brought to life the age of addiction in which we now live? A wide-open supply tap is vital to the answer, but it's not the whole story. For that, we need to factor in the extent to which our sociocultural context is driving us toward substances and behaviors that addict. Vast numbers of us are drawn to this form of hibernation we call *addiction* because when we look forward, we feel hopeless; when we look within, we find emptiness; when we look behind us, we see personal stories characterized by abuse, neglect, dysfunction, and regret—adversities that have left us deeply wounded—and, when we look around us, we find we're disconnected from others, detached from a sense of community and belonging, bereft of close relationships. We use drugs and alcohol, and we keep using them even when they start to do us serious harm because we're hurting, hopeless, empty, and alone. The same is true of gambling, porn, food, shopping, work, and more. The objects of addiction offer a dependable, immediate, and immersive alternative to the harsh reality of *life*.

In what has gone before, we have made ample use of words like "addiction," "addict," and "addicted." Before we go on, let's take a step back and define these well-worn terms.

PART TWO

UNDERSTANDING ADDICTION

Chapter 5

ENSLAVING SOLUTION

ADDICTUS

The emergence of the modern concept of addiction—what people think about when they think about addiction—owes much to the work of a physician from Philadelphia named Benjamin Rush. Born in 1745 as the fourth of seven children, Rush was something of a polymath. He graduated with a bachelor's degree from what is now Princeton University at the age of fourteen. Following a five-year apprenticeship under Dr. John Redman, Rush left the US to study medicine at the University of Edinburgh at twenty years of age. By the time he returned home, he had toured much of Europe and was fluent in French, Spanish, and Italian. A vigorous supporter of the American Revolution, Rush became a member of the Continental Congress and would place his signature on the US Declaration of Independence. He was a close friend of President John Adams and a politically active social reformer, opposing slavery and the death penalty and advocating for government-funded public schools and education for women. As a physician, Rush had a guiding influence on the emerging medical profession, championing the importance of hygiene to physical health and leading early work on the subject of mental illness. In 1965, the American Psychiatric Association described him as the "father of modern psychiatry."

Despite such diverse interests, Benjamin Rush was also the leading light of a public health campaign that warned against the perils of drinking hard liquor. Rush was no prohibitionist; beer and cider were, to his way of thinking, "wholesome" beverages that offered a healthy alternative to distilled alcoholic drinks like gin, rum, and whiskey.[1] His concern was with these "ardent spirits," which were as cheap and abundant in the US of the late eighteenth and early nineteenth centuries as they had been during London's earlier Gin Craze. Rush brought his expertise as a pioneer in the study of mental health to the campaign, contesting the view that drunkenness was a simple choice. Instead, he argued that the properties of alcohol itself could cause a person to lose control over the decision to drink.

Indeed, within the pages of *An Inquiry into the Effects of Ardent Spirits upon the Human Body and Mind with an Account of the Means of Preventing and of the Remedies for Curing Them*, published in 1805, we find the earliest description of addiction as a loss of control over the decision to drink.[2] In another pamphlet with a no-less-cumbersome title, Rush warned of the threat posed by addiction to wider society: "a people corrupted by strong drink," he forewarned, "cannot long be a free people."[3]

"Once there were no addicts," writes philosopher Kent Dunnington. "Or at least if there were, no one could have known it. The notion of the 'addict' and the corresponding concepts of addiction and addictive substances are of modern vintage. . . . The modern concept of addiction was worked out as a response both to these testimonies and to the exigencies of the burgeoning temperance movement."[4] This is true. However, the modern concept of addiction was not created ex nihilo in Benjamin Rush's Philadelphia study. Nor was it the invention of his contemporaries. Its roots go way back to the early Roman Republic of the fifth century BC.

In a 2019 article on the etymology of addiction, Richard Rosenthal, now a clinical professor of Psychiatry and Biobehavioral Sciences at David Geffen School of Medicine, UCLA, and Suzanne Faris delve deep into addiction's backstory.[5] The Twelve Tables, a series of legal definitions, rights, and procedures, inscribed on twelve bronze tablets and displayed publicly in Rome, formed the foundation of Roman law for a thousand years and have had a profound influence on contemporary notions of justice, punishment, equality, and property ownership. In legal proceedings, the Twelve Tables granted the *praetor urbanus* (the official in charge) the right to judge cases and determine punishments following an oft-rehearsed formula: "*do, dico, addico,*" which is best translated as, "I give, I say, I adjudge." In cases of unpaid gambling debts, if the *praetor urbanus* decreed that the debtor's punishment should be enslavement, the judicial act deployed was an *addictio*. The debtor, no longer in control of his own life, was handed over to his owner and became his *addictus* (slave). If the debt remained unpaid after a statutory sixty-day period, the *addictus* became the creditor's permanent property, to be "kept, killed, or sold as a common slave" at his discretion. According to Roman law, an *addictus* was neither a citizen nor a person.[6] The parallels between the Roman Republic's brutal justice and contemporary addiction experience are striking. In addiction, the individual experiences a loss of self-control and personal agency, often feeling like a slave to an external personal power. Addiction leaves suffering and deprivation in its wake. It undermines the addict's place in the community, destroying all sense of identity and inherent value. Ultimately, many of today's *addicti* are killed by their enslaver.

By the time of Christ, addiction language was used metaphorically, outside the judicial context, to describe the act of choosing to engage in self-destructive behavior, such as allowing sexual desire to run rampant. It was also deployed positively to refer to all-consuming devotion to a noble pursuit. The Roman statesman and lawyer Cicero (106–43 BC) described himself as being *addictum deditum* (bound and dedicated) to serve the interests of the Republic. The Stoic philosopher Seneca (c. 3 BC–AD 64) made regular use of the word *addicere* in his work, arguing that while some devoted themselves to carnal pleasures (*animum corpoi addixit*), the enlightened look beyond the superficial charms of the

Many of today's *addicti* are killed—if not physically then practically—by their enslaver.

physical world. According to Rosenthal and Faris, "What started as literal, the fate of the debt bondsman (*addictus*), under the ancient Law of the Twelve Tables, became metaphorical. . . . A behavior like gambling, which previously might have led someone to be sentenced to slavery, now *was* the enslavement. This was then expanded so that it was the pursuit of wealth or fame or even philosophy to which one was enslaved. In some instances, the goal itself was considered misguided; in others, it was the excessiveness of the pursuit."[7]

Today, we continue to use addiction language metaphorically. Negatively, it refers to a form of slavery—a state the enslaved person themselves co-conspires to create—to destructive impersonal forces, both substances and activities. Positively, in popular culture, addiction language is applied liberally to describe a sense of passion or commitment toward something. If you're really into something, you're "addicted" to it, whether it's a new flavor of soup, the latest bingeworthy TV show, or a fresh approach to getting in shape. "When marketers refer to a game, product, or activity as addictive or addicting, they mean that it's exciting and will sustain consumer interest. The name conveys desirability: it will meet your needs and is habit-forming (but in the nicest possible way)."[8]

CONTINUUM

Carlos, the Argentinian co-owner of a large and successful import-export business, has always been a heavy drinker. Still, recently things have deteriorated, leaving family and friends anxiously trying to find a way to help him before it's too late. A family friend says of Carlos, "He says he's not addicted, but his drinking is destructive and seems out of control. Is he in denial? How do we convince him to get help?"

If you take Carlos to an AA meeting, it's unlikely he'd be willing to take Step 1, accepting that he is "powerless over alcohol" and that his life has become "unmanageable." He argues that he goes for extended periods without drinking and functions well professionally. And yet, when he starts drinking, Carlos never stops at one or two. It appears he can't. A couple of years ago, he totaled a company vehicle, driving drunk, and was lucky to escape with his life and having done no one else severe harm. Despite the boozy culture within their family and friend group, everyone agrees that there is something "different" about how Carlos drinks. He is driven in the way he drinks and emotionally involved with alcohol in a way they are not.

Is Carlos addicted to alcohol? Despite our best efforts and the development of professional diagnostic criteria, addiction still isn't easy to diagnose.[9] "Addiction is an abstract concept, like love and fairness," explain Robert West and Jamie Brown.[10] "As a social construct, addiction has fuzzy boundaries."[11] No scan or blood test can diagnose addiction. Instead, as with most psychological and physical disorders, we diagnose addiction with reference to a set of symptoms, not by detecting an underlying pathology.[12] As such, sometimes—as in the case of Carlos and much to the chagrin of those trying to challenge an addict in denial—like beauty, addiction is found in the eye of the beholder.

In this context, it helps to view addiction as a continuum, ranging from mild to severe, rather than a binary state. Bruce Alexander explains:

> At the mild end of the continuum, addiction only occasionally overwhelms a person's life. . . . Mild forms of addiction may be short-lived (e.g., a short but all-consuming affair with a lover, cult, or drug), situational (e.g., gamblers who do not lose their money if they stay away from the racetrack), socially acceptable (e.g., a lucrative work addiction), episodic (in the case of a "binger"), or simply less than fully overwhelming. In the middle of the continuum, addicted people strive to maintain a "double life," which produces the appearance of normal psychosocial integration more or less successfully. At the severe end of the continuum, addiction can be totally overwhelming and unconcealable. The addicted person's previous lifestyle can be destroyed. Irrevocable harm can be inflicted on other people. The overwhelming involvement of addiction can reach an unrelenting, hellish intensity, and may have fatal consequences.[13]

RELENTLESS DESIRE

So what is addiction? Building on a careful analysis of the full range of modern addiction theories, psychologists Robert West and Jamie Brown of University College London argue that addiction is "a chronic condition involving a repeated powerful motivation to engage in a rewarding behavior, acquired as a result of engaging in that behavior, that has significant potential for unintended harm."[14] There are five elements to that definition. In what follows, we'll examine each one in turn. As we do so, we will lay a solid foundation for our thinking about addiction and all that we might do to help addicts in the realms of policy, prevention, treatment, and long-term support.

First, addiction is a chronic condition—it persists for an extended period of time or constantly recurs. If the behavior doesn't have a history, even a relatively brief one, it's not an addiction. Getting drunk every night on vacation doesn't make you an alcoholic. Getting carried away on a one-off visit to a casino, even if you do great harm to your bank balance, doesn't make you a gambling addict. Using drugs occasionally, even so-called "hard" drugs like heroin and crack, doesn't make you a drug addict.

> **Addiction is the inability to choose *not* to do something.**

Second, addiction involves a repeated powerful motivation that results in "abnormally and damagingly high priority" being given to the activity at the heart of the addiction.[15] This ongoing, intense motivation to engage in the activity may or may not line up with what, in the cold light of day, the addict genuinely desires. In addiction you don't always want what you want. That's why smokers continue to light up dozens of times a day despite the health risks and financial costs. It's why a porn addict will stay up late into the night even though they have a vital job interview the next morning. Addiction is the inability to choose *not* to do something. As a polysubstance addict in recovery, Judith Grisel says: "The opposite of addiction, I have learned, is not sobriety but choice. For many like me, drugs act as potent tools that obscure freedom."[16] In addiction, a seemingly unbridgeable gulf separates what we genuinely desire from what we actually pursue.

The relentless desire at the heart of addiction cannot be explained by simply pointing to "this" or "that" aspect of the person's psychology, physiology, social context, or spiritual state. It's much more complex than that. "The motivational system," West and Brown explain, "is the set of brain processes that energize and direct our actions; it shapes the flow of behavior on a moment-to-moment basis."[17] The motivational system involves our beliefs, motives, impulses, and inhibitions (urges), plans, emotions, and drives (say, thirst). Together, these elements produce actions (drinking a beer) and behavior patterns, such as the daily heavy drinking of an alcoholic.[18] In a healthy motivational system, these elements interact so that no particular motivational force dominates for an extended period of time. In addiction, the motivational system's balance is lost.

The motivational system can get out of whack for a variety of reasons. Some factors, such as anxiety, depression, low self-esteem, and impulsivity, are *internal* but unrelated to the addictive activity. Others, like habit formation, withdrawal symptoms, tolerance, and mood disturbance, are internal but exist as a direct result of the addictive activity. Yet others are *external* social and environmental factors, such as the strain of living in distressing circumstances, the unfettered opportunities created by a particular lifestyle, or peer pressure within a friend group. A personalized blend of these factors produces a motivational system that prioritizes, to an extreme and damaging degree, addictive behavior.[19]

PRIZED ASSET

For many years, residents who chose to abandon the program at Yeldall Manor would need to walk themselves and their belongings down the half-mile-long driveway and, from there, another couple of miles to the local train station in Twyford. A staff member would always walk that first half-mile alongside them, listening, encouraging, and quietly praying, hoping that the resident would turn back to confront whatever was driving the decision to leave. It occasionally worked, but more often than not, it didn't. Not long after I returned to Yeldall as a staff member, this practice stopped, and when a resident left the program prematurely, a staff member would drive them down to Twyford station. I recall one such journey with Henry, a tall Irishman in his late fifties, who'd spent decades addicted to heroin and methadone, a long-lasting synthetic opioid prescribed as a heroin substitute as part of maintenance therapy.

What made that journey stick in my mind was the fact that rather than claim to be ready to continue with recovery under his own steam— the standard position—Henry was quite sure that he was leaving to score. Focused but far from excited, Henry knew precisely what lay ahead and was in no mood to pretend otherwise.

The prized asset of addictive experiences is the capacity to eliminate pain.

Naïve but eager to encourage a change of mind, I challenged Henry. "No matter how good it will make you feel," I said, "that feeling won't last." Henry shot back, visibly irritated before I could get the words out of my mouth: "It's not going to feel good," he said. "I can't remember when it last felt good."

Addiction is a chronic condition involving a powerful motivation. The focus of this relentless desire, the axis of addiction, is a rewarding behavior (the third element of our definition). Whether the experience involves a substance or a behavior, it generates powerful brain changes that deliver some kind of "reward." Indeed, research demonstrates that activities like gambling and viewing pornography produce similar brain changes as those experienced by drug addicts.[20]

However, while the experience around which addiction and the life of the addict revolves is rewarding, we must distinguish between *reward* and *pleasure*. As Henry's comments illustrate, they are not the same thing. Pleasure is rarely the lasting appeal of the behavior. If anything, the opposite is true. The prized asset of addictive experiences is the capacity to eliminate pain, not provide pleasure.

Addictions begin as solutions to problems. They arrive as answers to unspoken prayers. They engage us in a whole-person experience that's profoundly rewarding because it meets, or masks, deep needs for things like inner peace, self-assurance, emotional soothing, life purpose, a sense of identity, tribal belonging, and spiritual experience. We develop such strong attachments to these experiences because the rewards they deliver are instantaneous and consistent.

One fallacy surrounding addiction is the belief that addicts always experience a "high"—a sense of euphoria or pleasure. Another is that addictive behavior always involves intoxication. Neither is true. Slaughtered, wasted, blotto, three sheets to the wind, loaded . . . the English language is replete with slang to describe being intoxicated, whether drunk or high. And yet, we would never apply any of these words to the person who, despite laws prohibiting smoking indoors, still manages to smoke sixty a day, or to the executive who works eighty hours, week after week, despite the warnings of their physician and the threats of their spouse. The rewards delivered by the addictive experience vary significantly between different people and different objects of addiction over time.

"Addicts turn to it out of negative motivations—fear, anxiety, guilt, discomfort—which the substance or involvement serves to lessen for a time," writes Stanton Peele, a pioneer in the study of addiction. "While they may have once had a pleasurable response to the object of addiction, that has long since faded into the background by the time they are addicted."[21] Judith Grisel makes the same point as she reflects on what motivated her drug use: "As with every addict, my days of actually getting 'high' were long past. My using was compulsive and aimed more at escaping reality than at getting off. I'd banged my head against the wall long enough to realize that nothing new was going to happen."[22]

OMINOUS DANCE

Fourth, addiction is acquired as a result of engaging in the behavior. You don't become a nicotine addict the moment you first take a drag of your friend's Marlboro or a gaming addict as soon as you set up a *World of Warcraft* account. Nor does addiction preexist in certain people or particular substances or activities. A person may be more or less vulnerable to addiction, and a substance or activity may be more or less likely to become an object of addiction. The potential is there, to differing degrees, on both sides of the equation. However, addictions only develop as subject and object interact—one drink, click, breath, roll, touch at a time. It's a step-by-step process—an ominous dance—that moves so slowly that the onset of addiction is hard to perceive, let alone arrest.

It's worth explicitly stating that you can use addictive substances and engage in addictive behaviors of all kinds without becoming addicted. Opioids are commonly prescribed for postoperative pain control, and the vast majority of patients cease using them as soon as their pain subsides. Likewise, many people use opioids to manage chronic pain without becoming addicted. Although 57 percent of the world's population does not drink alcohol—a higher figure than one might expect—the majority of those who do, do so without becoming addicted.[23] The same is true of potentially addictive activities. For countless people, sex is a source of pleasure and intimacy. Each day, millions gamble without getting into any kind of trouble. Carl Hart, a professor of both psychology and psychiatry at Columbia University, brings firsthand experience of drug use, as well as academic rigor, to his work. "To meet the most widely accepted definition of addiction—the one in psychiatry's *Diagnostic and Statistical Manual of Mental Disorders*, or DSM—a person's drug use must interfere with important life functions like parenting, work, and intimate relationships. The use must continue despite

95

ongoing negative consequences, take up a great deal of time and mental energy, and persist in the face of repeated attempts to stop or cut back . . ." And yet, Hart observes, "more than 75% of drug users—whether they use alcohol, prescription medications, or illegal drugs—do not have this problem. Indeed, research shows repeatedly that such issues affect only 10–25% of those who try even the most stigmatized drugs, like heroin and crack."[24]

Fifth, the behavior at the center of addiction must have significant potential for unintended harm. If it doesn't, it might be a good old-fashioned bad habit or, maybe, an unhealthy attachment, but it's not an addiction.

Harm is central to the definition of substance use disorder (SUD) in the latest version of the *Diagnostic and Statistical Manual of Mental Disorders* (DSM-5), published by the American Psychiatric Association. SUD involves "patterns of symptoms caused by using a substance that an individual continues taking despite its negative effects." The DSM lists eleven potential symptoms, dividing them into four basic categories: impaired control, physical dependence, social problems, and risky use.[25]

> Addictions do immense harm to the body, mind, spirit, and relationships.

Addictions do immense harm to the body, mind, spirit, and relationships. In all likelihood, they take a toll on all those areas. Tragically, addiction tends to exacerbate the very problems that, at first, the experience resolved, soothed, or prevented. "Our addictions make promises they cannot keep," writes Timothy McMahan King. "They mimic solutions as opposed to providing them."[26]

This is where I believe some people stretch addiction language too far, diluting its meaning and doing unintended harm in the process. If everything is an addiction, then nothing is an addiction. This is becoming increasingly common, and, as a result, our exploration of both addiction proper and other related, though distinct, conditions are impoverished. In his influential book *Addiction and Grace*, Gerald May defines addiction as "any compulsive, habitual behavior that limits the freedom of human desire" and includes housekeeping, calendars, punctuality, popcorn, bridges, snakes, and writing on his extensive list of potential addictions.[27] There is an instructive connection between addiction and the "unhealthy attachments" May describes. However, the potential for harm posed by these objects and activities is simply too limited to justify describing them as addictions. Rather than conflating terms and concepts, removing important nuance from our language and thinking, we would be better served by the language of "unhealthy attachment," "bad habit," and "phobia" to describe some of what, today, is labeled as addiction. All addictions may be unhealthy attachments, but not all unhealthy attachments are addictions.

TOLERANCE & WITHDRAWAL

Despite their centrality to many historical and contemporary definitions of addiction, we have not said anything about withdrawal symptoms and tolerance. Why? Simply because what is also known as physiological adaptation or physical dependence is not an essential feature of addiction. That's not to say that it's not a common nor powerful feature of many substance addictions. In fact, the physical dangers associated with both opioid and alcohol addictions relate to physiological adaptation. Alcoholics should not stop drinking suddenly outside of the context of a medically managed detox due to the potentially fatal side effects of sudden alcohol withdrawal. Tragically, many heroin addicts overdose when relapsing after a period of "clean time," having overestimated their tolerance. A spike in overdoses often follows in the wake of a new batch of heroin, of greater purity or laced with fentanyl, hitting the streets.

You can, however, have addiction without physiological

adaptation. A gambling addict can become utterly overwhelmed by the desire to risk significant sums on events outside his control, placing his family's financial security in jeopardy, but experience no physical symptoms whatsoever if he is unable to act on that desire. Likewise, one can experience physiological adaptation without addiction. If your physician prescribes you an opioid painkiller, such as Tramadol or Codeine, for more than five days, you may experience withdrawal symptoms such as insomnia, sweating, diarrhea, and headaches—even if you show no signs of having developed an unhealthy relationship with your medication. Similarly, though you may suffer a mild headache if you don't get your morning coffee, you probably aren't addicted to caffeine. For most of us, coffee drinking is a habit—not a bad habit, just a habit—and your body has adapted to its regular morning caffeine hit. However, your coffee drinking has no potential for causing harm, and your motivational system has not prioritized caffeine consumption to a damaging degree.

This position lines up with research summarized by Jim Orford, Professor of Clinical and Community Psychology at the University of Birmingham, who notes that "laboratory studies have clearly shown the existence of withdrawal symptoms on the cessation of caffeine intake. . . . [However] caffeine appears to have only weak stimulant effects on mood . . . and [there is] no convincing evidence that people feel their intake of caffeine to be out of control, nor that they become preoccupied with caffeine use to the point of neglecting other roles or activities, nor that people continue to take caffeine despite knowing that they have health problems that are aggravated by it, nor that people try to stop taking it and have difficulty doing so."[28]

This, then, is addiction: a modern concept with a rich history; an abstract concept that refers to an all too concrete and painful reality; and a complex condition that straddles a continuum of severity. Addiction is an enslaving solution. As we will now see, addiction is also a best friend, a constant companion, and a lover.

Chapter 6

TOXIC RELATIONSHIP

"MY WIFE WAS HEROIN"

In the summer of 2009, after three years leading an international church in Santa Cruz, our first stint in Bolivia was drawing to a close. Inspired by the work of a local ministry to street teenagers—Operation Restoration, where I volunteered to improve my Spanish—my wife and I planned to establish a home for adults with addiction issues. We built a relationship with Dunklin Memorial Camp, a renowned addiction ministry in Florida, and planned to adapt its "Cities of Refuge" model for the Bolivian context. This vision felt right, the plans achievable, and our field research indicated that the need was genuine and urgent.

And yet, when the time came to step out and share the vision widely, we felt a check in our spirits. It was a strange feeling. It didn't feel like we'd been on the wrong path—far from it—but the assurance we needed to press what, in my mind's eye, was a big green *Launch* button just wasn't there. So, perplexed but at peace, we let it lie. Four years later, to our surprise and amazement, God began speaking about Bolivia again. The issue hadn't been the essential vision, it was the timing. Novō Communities was established in 2015 with a vision to bring new life to individuals, peace to families, and hope to communities gripped by addiction.

In the fall of 2009, with the door then shut to addiction ministry in Bolivia, I reached out to Ken Wiltshire, Director of Yeldall Manor, to ask about employment opportunities. Ken had cut his teeth in leadership on London's Fleet Street, serving as a workers' union steward for a national newspaper. He moved to Yeldall in the mid-1980s, where for nearly thirty years, his soft heart and hard feet impacted the lives of hundreds of men seeking freedom from addiction. By 2009, Ken was past statutory retirement age and struggling with his health. Succession planning was underway, and to my surprise, I was offered a role that would prepare me to assume the leadership of the organization. By the spring of 2010, we were back in our cottage in Waltham St. Lawrence, a commuter village west of London, preparing for five of the most fulfilling years of my working life—years marked by rich relationships and deep learning about addiction, recovery, and leadership.

Like the iris of the human eye—indeed, like any relationship—no two addictions are the same.

The indomitable Marcus Foy was one of my many teachers among Yeldall's staff and residents. A proud Londoner, Marcus was himself in recovery and served as a therapist, working one-to-one with a caseload of residents and leading therapeutic groups. My introduction to Marcus came through a just-released promotional film aimed at prospective residents in prisons, hospitals, and the community. It opened with a montage in which ex-residents looked back on life in addiction. When his turn came, Marcus delivered the kind of pithy line for which, I soon discovered, he had a rare gift. "First and foremost, my wife was heroin," he said, "but crack became the girlfriend and the excitement of [drugs]."

> **Addiction is an intense, all-consuming, and ultimately toxic relationship.**

What is addiction? Having replied to that question with a definition, I now want to offer a different kind of answer. It's one you often hear on the lips of addicts themselves. Addiction is an intense, all-consuming, and ultimately toxic relationship.

LOVE STORY

Marcus was the first person I heard describe their addiction in relational terms, but he would by no means be the last. Similar comparisons are a recurring theme in the testimonies and memoirs of addicts of all stripes. The title of Caroline Knapp's vivid memoir says it all—*Drinking: A Love Story*. Knapp, an Ivy League graduate and award-winning journalist, died at age forty-two from complications due to lung cancer, having smoked since her early twenties, but it was alcohol that would shape her life most profoundly. "When you're drinking," she writes, "liquor occupies the role of a lover or a constant companion. It sits there on its refrigerator shelves or on the counter or in the cabinet like a real person, as present and reliable as a best friend."[1]

William Cope Moyers, the eldest son of journalist and former White House Press Secretary Bill Moyers, describes his addiction similarly: "Cocaine was my running buddy, my soul mate, my faithful lover, my reliable colleague, my fun-loving playmate who tagged along everywhere I went. Alcohol and cocaine were always there for me, they never let me down."[2]

In her memoir, the journalist Ann Marlowe explores the power dynamics of her relationship with heroin.

While heroin has been compared with a lover in countless songs and stories, it isn't quite. You might come to heroin seeking control, looking for a relationship where you wouldn't get hurt, and indeed you find a lover who will never abandon you. But oddly enough, speculate as you will about quitting, you can only hurt yourself, never the drug. Heroin will not listen to you, not even once, but it will always take you back. It will be there, waiting, whenever you are ready to return. . . . The real risk in two-person relationships is unexpected, the sudden failure of trust. And while heroin bags are fungible, an affair you can abandon or pick up at any time with no difference in feeling, the power and devastation of romantic love spring from the uniqueness of the loved one. If you lose him, there will never, never be a true replacement.[3]

What is it that these relationships offer? Remember, addiction has much in common with hibernation. It's a way of adapting to life in a hostile habitat where vital physical, emotional, relational, and spiritual needs have gone unmet. In some cases, these underlying needs are felt, understood, and articulated by the individual. In many others, they're a total mystery to the person laid low by them. Like the iris of the human eye—indeed, like any relationship—no two addictions are the same. The benefits derived from them are deeply personal.

However, the more you listen to addiction stories, the more it becomes clear that what addictions always do is meet a person at the place where life has left them most vulnerable. The warm glow that comes when you anticipate, let alone sip, your first "wine o'clock" drink may be a tonic to anxiety and weariness. The adrenaline hit and sense of total immersion found in a high-stakes horse race may soothe a sense of impotence and despair. Endless hours playing *League of Legends* may deliver a feeling of self-esteem and tribal belonging in a virtual world, perhaps compensating crippling inadequacy or chronic loneliness. Heroin's supreme qualities as a painkiller may mask self-contempt and shame resulting from parental neglect, sexual abuse in childhood, or professional failure.

"Like patterns in a tapestry," writes Gabor Maté in *In the Realm of Hungry Ghosts*, "recurring themes emerge in my interviews with addicts: the drug as emotional anesthetic; as an antidote to a frightful feeling of emptiness; as a tonic against fatigue, boredom, alienation and a sense of personal inadequacy; as stress reliever and social lubricant. In places high and low these themes blight the lives of hungry ghosts everywhere."[4]

> Addictive behaviors make life in a dark world tolerable—until they don't.

SLEIGHT OF HAND

If human flourishing is defined in terms of material prosperity, life expectancy, and advances in industry and technology, we are indeed at the zenith of human history. However, the advent of the age of addiction should alert us to the fundamental damage modern society is doing to our mental, relational, and spiritual health. The habitat described in the preceding chapters is one within which it is hard to cope, let alone flourish. As such, increasing numbers embrace a means to enter a self-induced hibernation. Whether it's snorting ketamine, scrolling Pornhub, slavishly working, or scoring heroin, addictive behaviors make life in a dark world tolerable—until they don't. And then, they make it darker still.

Ahead of her time, Shirley Chisholm had it right. The first black woman elected to the United States Congress, in 1969, before a Select Committee of the House of Representatives, Chisholm forcefully declared: "A quality of life that creates a desire to be alienated from it, to escape from it . . . is responsible for the use of drugs. It is not heroin or cocaine that makes one an addict; it is the need to escape from a harsh reality."[5]

Neuroscientist Judith Grisel provides an arresting description of alcohol's capacity to both meet her felt needs and to unearth needs that, to that point, were hidden from her sight:

> The first time I got drunk, at thirteen, I felt as Eve should have after tasting the apple. Or as a bird hatched in a cage would feel upon being unexpectedly set free. The drug provided physical relief and spiritual antidote for the persistent restlessness I'd been unable to identify or share. An abrupt shift of perspective coincident with guzzling half a gallon of wine in my friend's basement somehow made me feel sure that both life and I were going to be all right. Just as light is revealed by darkness and joy by sorrow, alcohol provided powerful subconscious recognition of my desperate strivings for self-acceptance and existential purpose and my inability to negotiate a complex world of relationships, fears, and hopes. At the same time, it seemed to deliver, on a satin pillow, the key to all my blooming angst. Abruptly relieved from an existence both harsh and lackluster, I had finally discovered ease. Or perhaps that ease was more akin to anesthesia, but at the time and for several years after I not only couldn't tell the difference but didn't care. . . . Though I never achieved the overwhelming sense of wholeness that I experienced the first time, alcohol continued to confer muted contentment . . ."[6]

It was love at first sight for Grisel. She could never recapture the overwhelming sense of wholeness that accompanied her first joyous experiences of drunkenness. Nevertheless, alcohol captured her heart because its all-encompassing embrace felt so good.

It's striking that Grisel describes her drinking, first and foremost, as a means of nullifying *negatives*, not attaining *positives* such as peace, hope, healing, and joy. Alcohol's sleight of hand obscured feelings of emptiness, meaninglessness, and angst, and its gentle whispers silenced inner voices peddling self-doubt and fear. At the bottom of a glass, she found an escape hatch from despair, emptiness, and complexity. But, of course, it wouldn't last. Before long, alcohol would deliver her into the heart of darkness, unexpected freedom morphing into inescapable bondage. Ann Marlowe observes, "It is the absence of pain that you are looking for, but the absence of living that you get."[7]

FALSE GOD

So far, the relationships to which we've likened addiction are human relationships. In the objects of their addiction, the addict experiences something analogous to a relationship with a wife, lover, friend, colleague, or therapist. These relationships engage us emotionally, physically, psychologically, and spiritually. Indeed, the whole-life nature of addiction explains why addiction treatment works best when it engages the whole person, not just one element of the whole. Psychological work, for example, will prove of limited value if a vital physiological issue (such as chronic pain or malnourishment) is not addressed. Similarly, spiritual work will bear little in the way of lasting fruit if social factors, such as loneliness or an abusive relationship, are not tackled effectively.

Philosopher Kent Dunnington, whom we'll meet toward the end of this book, argues that addiction should also be compared to a spiritual relationship with a higher power. In fact, he goes further, describing addiction as a form of idolatry. "Addiction is—like all sin—a form of idolatry because it elevates some proximate good to the status of ultimate good, a status that belongs to God alone."[8] Like all idols, addiction turns heads because the false god promises to meet our deepest needs—for things like security, certainty, significance, connection, and purpose.

"Addiction is uniquely alluring, uniquely captivating, and uniquely powerful because its object comes so close to making good on its false promise to be God," he continues. "All sin is an attempt to overreach our powers and to establish on our own a flourishing and fulfillment that can only be found within right relationship to God. . . . Major addiction is not necessarily the most tempting form of idolatry; it is too extreme, totalizing, and demanding to tempt many of us. But exactly because it is so extreme, totalizing, and demanding, addiction is the most potent form of idolatry on offer."[9] Dunnington's description lines up with what I've heard from those who've shared their addiction stories with me.

Gerald May makes precisely the same point. "Spiritually, addiction is a deep-seated form of idolatry. The objects of our addictions become our false gods. These are what we worship, what we attend to, where we give our time and energy instead of love. Addiction, then, displaces and supplants God's love as the source and object of our deepest true desire."[10]

Painfully aware that his relationship with alcohol had become an all-consuming affair, my friend Mark concluded that he needed to reaffirm his vows to Jenny, his wife, who had watched his slow slide into addiction and supported him through twelve months of residential treatment from a distance. His addiction, Mark believed, had been both adulterous and idolatrous. "I was unfaithful to Jenny, and to God, replacing them with alcohol, living my life in an addictive cycle of dependency."[11]

As we sat by the fire talking one evening at Yeldall Manor, my friend Gareth, back in treatment after years spent working as a recovery pastor in a thriving local church, felt he had strayed so far from God, so deeply into the realm of darkness, that he was convinced that he needed to be baptized as a believer for a second time. To his mind, the darkness of the spiritual experiences that accompanied his latest prolonged relapse demonstrated that he had not simply strayed far from God; he'd worshiped at the feet of an idol.

> Unchecked, this fire of relentless desire burns up everything in its path.

Like a passionate love affair, the all-consuming relationship we call addiction is a potent force. No matter how the flame starts, once the fires of addiction are burning, they are not easily extinguished. They take on a life of their own. Unchecked, this fire of relentless desire burns up everything in its path until, be it sooner or later, it burns itself and its host out.

Our next task is to explore what creates this nearly-unstoppable force for self-harm and the destruction of families, communities, and societies. What's going on inside the mind of a person who cannot choose *not* to do something that they want to choose not to do?

Chapter 7

THE APPARATUS
OF ADDICTION

SIMON

The ancient city of Canterbury is the spiritual heart of the county of Kent, known as "the garden of England," in the southeasternmost corner of the British Isles. It is also home to the archbishop of Canterbury, the principal leader of the Church of England and the spiritual leader of the 85-million-strong worldwide Anglican Communion. Five miles to the north of Canterbury, the River Thames flows eastward, out of London, to meet the salty waters of the North Sea. Twenty miles to its south, the Strait of Dover creates a narrow-yet-elemental divide between Great Britain and continental Europe, a historic buttress against military aggression and an enduring barrier to cultural integration.

The setting for Chaucer's fourteenth-century classic *The Canterbury Tales*, Canterbury Cathedral has drawn Christian pilgrims since the martyrdom of Archbishop Thomas Becket (d. 1170) by knights acting on the orders of King Henry II. Today, the cathedral attracts visitors from around the globe drawn by a rich story that dates to pre-Roman times and the arrival of Christianity with St. Augustine, the "apostle to the English."

My own visits to Canterbury have been motivated by contemporary tragedies, not historical dramas. The first, back in 1999, was for a gathering of the International Substance Abuse and Addiction Coalition (ISAAC), a network of Christians who seek to connect, encourage, and equip one another as, in diverse settings, they strive to set captives free from addiction. The second, in January 2011, was to mourn the tragic loss of a young man named Simon Day.

In an interview with *The Times* of London, Simon's mother, Rachel, described Simon's journey into addiction, a relationship that got serious quickly and demanded an exclusivity that pulled Simon ever further away from family, friends, and his very sense of self. Simon started smoking cannabis at about the age of fifteen.[1] "He got into skateboarding and started going out a lot more," his mother explained. "There was a change in attitude. We didn't argue, but he didn't seem to want to be around us. I just put it down to him being a teenager. I didn't know drugs were behind it at that point." Despite being one of the top students for most subjects, Simon's grades deteriorated dramatically, and he left school at sixteen with just two basic qualifications.

After a year of a business studies course, Simon went to the University of Creative Arts in Canterbury, where he formed a band, *The Liaisons*. Simon's drug use soon took a darker turn. He started using ketamine. "He said it was a party drug, totally nonaddictive," Rachel told *The Times*. "I don't think anyone knew much about it then. It did him the most terrible physical damage, particularly to his bladder. I once walked past him in town and didn't recognize him because he was shuffling along like an old man. In the end, he could not go for more than ten minutes without needing the toilet.

The pain was dreadful. Once, on a car journey, we got stuck in a traffic jam when he needed to go, and he was howling and keening like a dog. Nothing seemed to ease it except more ketamine—until he found heroin."

Simon arrived at Yeldall Manor in the fall of 2010, a twenty-three-year-old with pallid skin and a withdrawn countenance. Trudging through an opioid detox and struggling to settle, his early weeks with us were extremely tough. Then faint signs of hope—recovery's most valuable commodity—appeared. Light returned to Simon's eyes and a hesitant smile to his face. He began to engage seriously with his counselor and in therapeutic groups. Against the odds, Simon completed his detox and, soon after, Rachel and Andy (Simon's dad) visited and connected with a beloved son who, for so many years, had been lost to his relationship with drugs. Things were going well.

And then, suddenly, everything changed. Simon and another resident decided to abandon the program together. Peers with more recovery experience tried to persuade him to stay and think things over. I can't remember a stronger "push" from the residents than the one to try to keep Simon from leaving. In the end, he left and immediately relapsed.

Simon spent Christmas with his family and then agreed to meet his dad on New Year's Eve for coffee at 11 a.m. at a Starbucks in Canterbury. Andy wanted to invite Simon to ring in the new year with the rest of the family at Simon's grandparents' home. Andy arrived on time and waited, but Simon didn't show up. Not that this was unusual. Experience told Andy that Simon was likely using with friends and had forgotten about coffee. What Andy didn't know was that Simon's friends hadn't seen him either. Over the next few days, Andy and Rachel tried in vain to contact Simon.

On January 2, with still no sign of Simon, his housemates forced their way into his room, where they found him dead. The inquest that followed concluded that Simon had overdosed on New Year's Eve.

When Andy and Rachel went to clear out his room, they found virtually all his possessions gone, even his guitar. His room was almost empty. Everything had been sold to pay for heroin.

The few items that remained spoke to a young man still trying to hold on to life and love beyond addiction: a silver ring, identical to one worn by Andy; a watch, a Christmas present from his parents that Rachel now wears; and a little white teddy bear Simon had loved as a child.

His room was almost empty. Everything had been sold to pay for heroin.

Early in January, a group of staff and residents from Yeldall drove down to Simon's funeral at St. Mary Bredin Church, Canterbury. It was a cold, overcast morning, and the traffic was heavy. We arrived just moments before the service began to find the church packed, a demonstration of the love and care of the family and friends that surrounded Simon. His grandfather, a former archbishop of Canterbury, did not officiate at the funeral. "On that day," Rachel explained, "he just wanted to be Granddad."

Looking back on their attempts to help Simon, Rachel gave voice to a sense of powerlessness and self-doubt that will be familiar to anyone who has tried to support a loved one in addiction. "I tried to love him out of it; Andy tried to shake him out of it," she said. "We did everything we could, but we still don't know if we did enough or if we did the right thing. When you discover your child is taking drugs, you're suddenly faced with a problem you have no idea how to sort out, but the truth is that, however hard you try, it is the addict who really has to want to change. Simon wanted to give up . . . but the call of drugs and of the lifestyle was too strong."

LEARNING PROCESS

Simon Day of Canterbury and Adam Johnson of Huntington (whom we met in chapter 2): two young men first crippled, then destroyed, by addiction; two young men who left unfathomable hollows in the lives of those who loved them; two young men fearfully and wonderfully made by the God who loved them dearly; two young men whose stories, in the age of addiction, are representative of countless more. Why couldn't they just stop?

To answer that question, we must dig deeper, turning our attention to the biological apparatus of addiction, the awesome and mysterious organ we call the brain. A foray into the neuroscience of addiction will help us understand why it is so hard for the addicted to stop, even when the costs of the addictive behavior so clearly outweigh the benefits. Similarly, clarity about what's going on inside the addicted brain will help us understand what's involved in establishing and sustaining life in recovery. Such understanding is vitally important for all seeking to help those gripped by addiction—friends, pastors, professionals, and addiction treatment providers—as well as families, like Simon's, trying to make sense of the "insanity" of addiction.

"I had come to believe I was insane because I did so many things I didn't want to do," confesses one of the contributors to *The Big Book* of Alcoholics Anonymous. "I didn't want to neglect my children. I loved them, I think, as much as any parent. But I did neglect them. I didn't want to get into fights, but I did get into fights. I didn't want to get arrested, but I did get arrested. I didn't want to jeopardize the lives of innocent people by driving an automobile while intoxicated, but I did."[2]

Two hundred years before St. Augustine arrived in Canterbury (AD 597) on his mission to bring the gospel to the English, another St. Augustine—this one from Hippo, modern-day Algeria—began writing *Confessions*, one of early Christianity's most influential texts.

Augustine wrote *Confessions* (the very first autobiography by a Christian) while in his early forties. He describes his early life as "a slave to lust" and the conversion to Christianity by which he would be "healed."[3] At one point in his reflections, Augustine gives voice to how he felt on hearing about the deep sense of liberty the philosopher Marius Victorinus experienced upon giving his life to Christ. He contrasts this with feeling controlled by powerful forces within himself that don't reflect his most genuine desires—and the process by which he became enslaved by them. "I sighed after such freedom," he recalls, "but was bound not by an iron imposed by anyone else but by the iron of my own choice. . . . By servitude to passion, habit is formed, and habit to which there is no resistance becomes necessity. By these links, as it were, connected one to another . . . a harsh bondage held me under restraint."[4] The degree to which Augustine's description aligns with modern neuroscience's understanding of how addictions form and function is quite remarkable. Choices ("servitude to passion") become habits ("habit is formed") that become compulsions ("necessity") that leave the individual unable to choose not to do things that are causing them great harm ("a harsh bondage held me under restraint").

Marc Lewis, a neuroscientist and retired professor of developmental psychology at the University of Toronto, who tells his own story of addiction and recovery in *Memoirs of an Addicted Brain* and *The Biology of Desire*, writes: "Addiction is the result of a natural learning process that has gone way too fast and way too far, yielding habits that are extremely difficult to 'unlearn.'"[5] Addictions come to life through "the motivated repetition of the same thoughts and behaviors until they become habitual."[6] Once established, these habits are extremely difficult to break because the learning process has hardwired the brain to view the addictive experience as something that delivers satisfying, immediate, and consistent rewards.

114

Lewis explains how this "hardwiring" occurs and why addictive habits are so difficult to disrupt even when we're desperate to break them.

> Addiction develops—it's learned—but it's learned more deeply and often more quickly than most other habits, due to a narrowing tunnel of attention and attraction. A close look at the brain highlights the role of desire in this process. The neural circuitry of desire governs anticipation, focused attention, and behavior. So the most attractive goals will be pursued repeatedly, while other goals lose their appeal, and that repetition (rather than the drugs, booze, or gambling) will change the brain's wiring. . . . Addiction is unquestionably destructive, yet it is also uncannily normal: an inevitable feature of the basic human design. That's what makes it so difficult to grasp—socially, scientifically, and clinically. . . . Addiction can therefore be seen as a developmental cascade, often foreshadowed by difficulties in childhood, always boosted by the narrowing of perspective with recurrent cycles of acquisition and loss. Like other developmental outcomes, addiction isn't easy to reverse because it rides on the restructuring of the brain. Like other developmental outcomes, it arises from neural plasticity, but its net effect is a reduction of further plasticity, at least for a while.[7]

STUCK IN A RUT

Once you leave the towns and cities, most of eastern Bolivia's roads are made of dirt or sand that need regular grading. If not, as traffic goes back and forth, it cuts tracks into the roads' surface that soon turn into deep, muddy ruts, particularly in the rainy season. For drivers, these tracks can present a real challenge. To a point, they're no problem. You simply let the car follow the tracks left by others. However, once the ruts get too deep, your vehicle can get stuck in the mud or "beached" on the strip of dirt that runs down the middle of the tracks. In these conditions, drivers must choose their course with care, avoiding these narrow channels because it's almost impossible to get back out once you're in them. Like heavy vehicles going back and forth along a dirt road, the learning process that produces addiction cuts ruts of habitual thinking and action that are difficult to escape, and once out, desperately easy to slip back into.

The developmental-learning model of addiction offers several insights that will help us understand and help those struggling to get free from addiction's hold.

First, addiction doesn't involve the brain being "hijacked" by hostile substances. It's not the substances consumed that change the brain; it's the experiences those substances provoke and our response to them. That's why activities such as gambling or watching pornography are also addictive. They don't expose us to "demon drugs" that overpower us. They elicit potent brain-changing experiences. Lewis puts it this way:

> Brain changes are not caused by booze or drugs. They result from having a string of similar experiences. Nice experiences. Experiences of relief. Experiences that feel good, or at least better than the rest of your boring and depressing life. These brain changes are caused by motivated repetition—repetition of something special—and how the brain responds to it. The powerful experiences that get the ball rolling are simply events that affect us deeply. Because they are engaging. Because they mean something. As they become even more meaningful, the corresponding brain changes gather more momentum, building on themselves, digging their own ruts—rainwater in the garden.[8]

Why do some substances and activities seem to lead to addiction more readily and quickly? The answer is found in the depth of the experience induced and the speed with which the experience is delivered. Hence, the short, intense highs produced by a crack pipe are far more likely to give rise to addiction and do so quickly than the gentle relief provided by a glass of Cabernet Sauvignon.

Second, while the brain is the fulcrum of all addictions, it doesn't function in isolation from our lived experience. The sociocultural factors we explored above, particularly adverse childhood experiences, prime the pump for addiction. In a dynamic relationship with our personalities, choices, and genetics, our experiences conspire to create our thirst for the kinds of rewarding experiences that, with "motivated repetition," change the brain and produce the habits of thought and action we call addictions. In other words, the depth of my need for, and orientation toward, powerful experiences of relief, escape, empowerment, control, meaning, and pleasure, is heavily influenced by my immediate context and life experience. For example, the relief and sense of inclusion provided by a joint smoked with a new group of friends will profoundly impact an anxious teenager desperately trying to find his feet in a new school, having just moved in with yet another new foster family. That same joint will have quite a different meaning when smoked by a secure postgraduate student settling down for a quiet night in with her devoted husband. As we have seen, heroin in the hands of servicemen stationed far from home, with "nothing to lose" and enduring the horrors of war, offers something that, when home on US soil, no longer seems so appealing.

Third, the *naturalness* of the learning process explains why each of us is vulnerable to developing unhealthy habits and addictions in

> Sociocultural factors, particularly adverse childhood experiences, prime the pump for addiction.

the first place. Addiction, as it is often said, is no respecter of persons. The same human capacities that enable us to form *good habits*, automating activities and releasing our conscious attention for learning new skills and higher-order thinking, work just as effectively at forming *bad habits*. The neuroplasticity that allows us to mature through the life stages of infancy, childhood, and adolescence, and then learn new skills and continue developing throughout adulthood, stands ready to zero in on the pursuit of any experience that meets our needs effectively and quickly.

Fourth, the brain change produced by "motivated repetition of the same thoughts and behaviors until they become habitual" is real and enduring.[9] These neurological changes make addictive patterns something altogether different from a set of "preferences" or simple "choices." Ann Graybiel, an Institute Professor in the Department of Brain and Cognitive Sciences at the Massachusetts Institute of Technology, has been at the forefront of brain research for over forty years. "Habits," she explains, "never really disappear. They're encoded into the structures of our brain, and that's a huge advantage for us because it would be awful if we had to relearn how to drive after every vacation. The problem is that your brain can't tell the difference between bad and good habits, and so if you have a bad one, it's always lurking there, waiting for the right cues and rewards."[10]

The permanence of brain change makes recovery difficult and punishment a blunt instrument in the fight against addiction (and, with it, against addiction-adjacent crime). It explains why early recovery needs to be worked out in safe places and safe communities, like rehabs and sober houses; why relapse is so common; and why, even decades into recovery, there remains the need to stay vigilant to anything that might trigger a return to the addictive behavior. Decades after he got clean, Marc Lewis's relationship with drugs has not been entirely forgotten.

You could say that my life became too full even to consider
a return to drugs, but that wouldn't tell the whole story.
Not at all. The sculpting of synapses in my early twenties is
irrevocable. The meaning of drugs, the imagined value they
represent, is still inscribed on my orbitofrontal cortex; and a
resonant flair of dopamine can still be ignited in my ventral
striatum, at least to some degree. These are the conditions
of my nervous system, and they are not reversible. As is
well known in the addiction lore, there is no final cure, just
recovery, abstention, and self-awareness.[11]

Fifth and finally, the brain change that drives addiction is not
determinative. "Habits aren't destiny," as Charles Duhigg puts it.[12]
Addiction significantly diminishes neuroplasticity, but it does not
destroy it. As such, the brain is always able to learn new, good, re-
covery-friendly habits of thought and action. It's not easy, especially
at first, but with time, discipline, and support, it is entirely possible
to create new tracks in the road that lead us forward while avoiding
the deep ruts of addiction.[13] "Neuroplasticity is the brain's natural
starting point for any learning process," writes Marc Lewis. "This
includes the development of addiction, of course. But it's also the
springboard to recovery. . . . People learn addiction through neuroplasticity, which is how they learn everything. They maintain their
addiction because they lose some of that plasticity. . . . Then, when
they recover . . . their neuroplasticity returns. Their brains start
changing again—perhaps radically."[14]

DOPAMINE & DESIRE

It is well known that the neurotransmitter dopamine plays a vital
role in addiction. However, contrary to popular understanding informed by the neuroscience of the 1950s and '60s, dopamine isn't a

"feel-good" or "pleasure chemical." This idea is founded on the assumption that *wanting* something and *liking* something is the same thing—an idea challenged back in the '80s by Kent Berridge and his team at the University of Michigan.[15]

In a series of experiments on rats, Berridge explored the role of dopamine in their relationship with sweet substances. Three scenarios were explored. In the first, a standard rat was given access to a sugary solution. As you might expect, the rat consumed copious amounts of the solution and showed all the telltale signs of rat pleasure as it did so. In the second scenario, while free access to the sugary solution continued, Berridge removed the dopamine from the rats' brains. Without the dopamine in their brains, the rats stopped drinking the sugary solution, appearing to confirm the fact that without dopamine, the brain cannot experience pleasure. However, the third scenario was the game changer. Again, the dopamine was removed from the rats' brains, but rather than just being given access to the sugary substance, the rats were force-fed the sugary substance.

Desire, not pleasure, is the heart of addiction.

What happened? The rats displayed all the signs of unadulterated pleasure as they drank, despite the absence of dopamine. Dopamine, it appears, is essential to the pursuit of pleasure. It is not essential to the experience of pleasure.

Berridge and his team had demonstrated precisely the same thing that a seasoned heroin addict like Henry (who we met earlier on the Yeldall driveway) will readily affirm. Just because you desperately want to do something, it doesn't mean you enjoy doing it. Dopamine is important to our understanding of addiction, but its role relates to the experience of desire and craving (*wanting*), not the experience of pleasure and attainment (*liking*). I can enjoy a cigarette without dopamine, but I will not feel the same craving to light up. With dopamine, long after I have ceased enjoying smoking, I will still have a strong desire to light up. The journalist David Edmonds unpacks the implications for addiction and recovery:

> For the addict, wanting becomes detached from liking. The dopamine system learns that certain cues—such as the sight of a coffee machine—can bring rewards. Somehow, in ways that are not fully understood, the dopamine system for the addict becomes sensitized. The wanting never goes away and is triggered by numerous cues. Drug addicts may find their urge to take drugs sparked by a syringe, a spoon, even a party, or being on a street corner . . . [making them] extremely vulnerable to relapse. They want to take the drugs again, even if the drugs give them little or no pleasure. For rats, the dopamine sensitization can last half a lifetime. The task now for researchers is to find whether they can reverse this sensitization—in rats, and then hopefully, in humans.[16]

Desire, not pleasure, is the heart of addiction. Gabor Maté puts it this way: "Addictions, even as they resemble normal human yearnings, are more about desire than attainment. In the addicted mode, the emotional charge is in the pursuit and the acquisition of the desired object, not in the possession and enjoyment of it. The greatest pleasure is in the momentary satisfaction of yearning."[17]

Bolivia's national anthem is an earnest, rousing, militaristic assertion of the nation's freedom. Its crescendo, a thrice-repeated line in the chorus, is a commitment to defend that freedom, fighting even to the death: "To die before we would live as slaves!" Each time I hear it, my mind turns to life in addiction and the hard road of recovery. Why do so many choose the slavery of addiction? The answer is that they don't. They learn it. And, having done so, like a pianist trying to "forget" how to play their instrument, they can't simply decide to "unlearn" it. A slower, more demanding, costlier process lies ahead.

In part one of this book, we explored the age of addiction, looking for the underlying causes on both the supply and demand sides of today's addiction epidemic. Those chapters sought to shed light on what drives the journey into addiction. In part two, our attention turned to trying to understand the mechanics and experience of life in addiction. Next, in part three, our focus shifts to the way out of addiction.

HOPE
IN
ADDICTION

Chapter 8

I CAN'T, BUT WE CAN

MOSES MOMENT

Her Majesty's Prison, Wormwood Scrubs, London, is an unlikely venue for what Huseyin Djemil describes as a "Moses moment" in his recovery journey. Standing in the shadow of its fort-like gatehouse, it's hard to believe that when "the Scrubs" opened in 1891, it was celebrated as a triumph of Victorian social reform, with provisions made for the health, welfare, and rehabilitation of offenders, not just their incarceration. The north–south alignment of its wings brought direct daylight into each cell at some point each day. Workshops for vocational training, recreational spaces, and a hospital were all constructed, as was a vast church, built—by the inmates themselves—to the design and standard of any contemporary Anglican parish church. (Portraits of the twelve apostles adorn the sanctuary walls, and legend has it that the face of Judas Iscariot bears an uncanny resemblance to the prison's first governor.) Today, despite being iconic in popular culture, having housed some of Britain's most notorious criminals, and appearing regularly in TV and film, Wormwood Scrubs is a forbidding place, its overcrowded wings beset by drugs and violence.

It's May 2003, and Huseyin is making his first visit to Wormwood Scrubs as Her Majesty's newly appointed Drug Strategy Coordinator for the London prisons. "It's my second week on the job," Huseyin explains as we talk over Zoom.[1] "I've got a suit on. I've got keys. I've got three or four prison officers around me, showing me around the prison, and I get to the closed-visit section, and I think, *I've been here before*. And it all just comes flooding back. I remember all this gore and blood, and I'm thinking, *Where is all this coming from?* I nearly lose it. I nearly start crying. I was senior enough that I could take a phone into a prison, so I whipped out my phone, and I decided I was going just to pretend to make a call. I said, 'Can you just give me a minute, guys?' And, standing there pretending to make a call, I think, *Come on, Huseyin, pull yourself together!*"

Only later did Huseyin realize what had triggered this abrupt and overwhelming flashback. As a young boy, he would visit his dad in the same closed-visit section of Wormwood Scrubs. On one occasion, as Huseyin sat patiently beside him, a family friend was stabbed in the head by another visitor. "I just remember seeing blood," says Huseyin, "seeing my dad going mad on the other side of the Perspex, not knowing what was going on."

Huseyin's return visit to the Scrubs has become a profoundly important milestone on a recovery journey and professional career that earned him a seat alongside government ministers and senior civil servants, shaping UK drug policy and helping others find freedom from slavery to addiction. "It felt like a Moses moment," he tells me. "In 1986, I left my area in disgrace. I had descended into chaos and was using crack and heroin every day. I was committing crime every day. My dad was dead. My mum died when I was in rehab. My friends thought I was dead. I owed drug dealers money. Isn't it amazing what God can do, even in one generation? Going from that little boy to that young man, with keys, a phone, in a suit, standing in that space, is really a credit to God. Obviously, I've lived my life, so I have something to do with it, but if it wasn't for Yeldall, if it wasn't for the relationship with God, if it wasn't for all the things that had been sown into me over the years . . . God is amazing."

Addiction doesn't have to be a life sentence.

Huseyin is living proof that addiction doesn't have to be a life sentence. His is a story to inspire those struggling to believe that life in recovery can be the rich and satisfying life (see John 10:10) that Jesus offers those who follow Him—a source of hope for all who are struggling to get free from the soul-destroying routines and diminishing returns that constitute addiction. Huseyin's life is an encouragement to those who are weary, despondent, and brokenhearted because a loved one is stuck in the straitjacket of addiction.

Huseyin's story is remarkable, but by no means is it unique. In 2016, John Kelly and colleagues from the Recovery Research Institute at Massachusetts General Hospital conducted a national study into the prevalence, pathways, and predictors of recovery from drug and alcohol problems. Their headline finding? Almost one in ten adults (9 percent) in the United States have resolved a substance abuse problem. Of these, 65 percent have been in recovery for five years or more, and 30 percent have been in recovery for more than fifteen years.[2] This is a remarkable story of hope! In fact, these are 22.35 million unique stories of hope, living proofs from across the ethnic and socioeconomic spectrum, related to all manner of substance addictions, reminding us that recovery *is* possible.

PROCESS OF CHANGE

The National Institute on Drug Abuse (NIDA), along with the Substance Abuse and Mental Health Services Administration (SAMHSA), defines recovery as "a process of change through which people improve their health and wellness, live self-directed lives, and strive to reach their full potential."[3] Recovery isn't a fixed state; it's a process. Recovery isn't a destination. If you're "in recovery," you're on a journey whose direction of travel is toward self-direction, health and well-being, and the fulfillment of your potential.

In *Addiction and Grace*, Gerald May observes that "addiction exists wherever persons are internally compelled to give energy to things that are not their true desires. . . . Addiction is a state of compulsion, obsession, or preoccupation that enslaves a person's will and desire. Addiction sidetracks and eclipses the energy of our deepest, truest desire for love and goodness."[4] In recovery, this state of compulsion is mastered. We develop the ability both to choose *not* to go after the addictive experience and to pursue a range of alternative priorities that align with the fundamental desires, beliefs, and values that represent who we want to be and what we want to do. In recovery, we stop allowing these desires to be trampled underfoot by the immediate rewards offered by the addictive behavior. As we do so, we experience a multiplicity of benefits related to our physical health, relationships, place in society, the inner world of our intellect and emotions, and our spiritual life. We develop a growing sense of positive momentum and purpose. The benefits ripple out to our family, friends, and the wider community. They flow down the generations, releasing children and children's children from the consequences of addiction.

This last point is vital. When we seek to measure the impact of recovery, doing a cost-benefit analysis on the expensive, draining, and often discouraging work of addiction treatment and recovery support, we need to do so from a vantage point that enables us to look over the horizon. Focusing on the individual and the here and now, we will find much to value and celebrate. As I write, my friend Rick, now seven years into recovery after multiple attempts at getting clean, is getting married. His life has been utterly transformed by the gospel and his recovery from addiction. But the story doesn't stop there. Alongside Rick today, celebrating his marriage to Rachel, are many others whose lives have been impacted by his recovery—by no means least, his teenage daughter.

Addiction stories are very often multigenerational. But so are recovery stories. Rick is employed, his relationships are stable, and he serves his church and the wider community. No longer is he tangled up with the criminal justice system. No longer is he in and out of detoxification wards and treatment programs. The impact of Rick's recovery—of every recovery—runs deep, far, and wide.

DEFEATING THE INDEFATIGABLE

The recovery process is rarely fast or straightforward, a reality that is hard to accept when faced with the suffering addiction leaves in its wake. There is, however, a real release that results from accepting the fact that addiction is a chronic disorder, and the pathways out are long, narrow, steep, and treacherous. As such, both lapses (brief slips) and relapses (prolonged returns to the addiction) are common. Recovery journeys rarely advance with the fast and certain rhythm of falling dominoes. Instead, like snakes and ladders, progress tends to be halting and precarious.

"Addictive desires," writes Kent Dunnington, "are indefatigably persistent . . . if the conflict between the will and nonaddictive desire (e.g., the desire for one too many pieces of cake) is a battle, then the conflict between the will and addictive craving is a war of attrition."[5] Recovering from addiction is hard. It demands sacrifice, patience, and grace from those in recovery and those who walk alongside them.

There is no one-size-fits-all when it comes to waging this war. John Kelly and the Research Recovery Institute explored the question of *how* people found lasting recovery in the research project cited above, making instructive discoveries. For example, 46 percent of the 22.35 million adults in recovery in the US today did so without any help beyond that offered by family and friends.[6] This phenomenon, known as "unassisted" or "natural" recovery, should not be overlooked. Indeed, it should be a source of encouragement. *Recovery is possible.* Indeed, it's possible even without professional help or participation in a mutual-help group like Alcoholics Anonymous or Narcotics Anonymous (NA).

One addict in recovery expressed his surprise on discovering an old friend had entered recovery without any form of assistance.

> I made contact with an old mate the other day. I genuinely thought he was dead, having not seen him since 1998. We used to use together: same stuff in the same way involving the same chaos. Much the same as myself, he used for over thirty years, mainly injecting heroin and cocaine at a rate of over £1,000 weekly. Six years ago he decided he had had enough and just stopped. He had never been on a script, never been in detox or rehab, and never been anywhere near a treatment service. All on his own, he has been totally abstinent for over six years, got a little fruit and vegetable store, and fixes motorcycles.[7]

Nevertheless, despite higher levels of unassisted recovery than we might expect, the majority (54 percent) of those in recovery in the US today took an "assisted recovery" pathway. Their profile suggests that those who took this pathway entered recovery with more severe and established addiction problems. They were more likely to have been using multiple substances, not just one; to list opioids as their primary substance, ahead of alcohol and cannabis; to have first used any substance before turning fifteen; to have a formal mental health or substance use disorder diagnosis; and to have been arrested. In short, the study suggested that the more severe the addiction, the less likely it is that recovery can be secured without significant external help.

What services had people in recovery used? More than one in four (28 percent) had entered into formal treatment such as a detox, rehab, or outpatient treatment program; 9 percent had used medication, such as Antabuse or Methadone; 22 percent had engaged with recovery support services such as a sober-living facility or a Recovery High School; 45 percent had been a part of mutual-help groups such as a twelve-step group, SMART Recovery, or Celebrate Recovery.[8] Of course, these services aren't mutually exclusive. Those questioned will have engaged with a constantly changing blend of different services over the years, benefiting from different things at different times as, one day at a time, they navigate life in recovery. Indeed, one of the benefits of thinking about recovery as a process or journey is the liberty it creates for a personalized approach where the focus is on engaging with a variety of inputs that help maintain positive forward momentum.

> In recovery, what are we recovering from? Is it solely the toxic, compulsive relationship with the addictive experience, or is there more to it?

IN RECOVERY, WHAT ARE WE RECOVERING FROM?

Gabor Maté issues a warning to those trying to understand why some people advance in recovery while others struggle to gain traction:

> It is useful to study and consider what combination of self-knowledge, strength, supportive environment, good fortune, and pure grace allows some people to escape the death grip of

hardcore addiction. . . . It is not helpful, however, to compare any one person with another. Just because one person succeeds doesn't mean that we're entitled to judge another for having failed. For all our similarities, we are each shaped by our own unique makeup and set of life experiences from the moment of conception. No two human brains look alike, not even those of identical twins. One person's pain cannot be compared with anyone else's, nor can we compare any two people's capacity to endure suffering.[9]

Maté also draws our attention to the variety of factors, some barely perceptible, that prove to be decisive. "In addition to the visible factors," he observes, "there are also many subtle, invisible ones that may positively influence our psychic strength and our capacity for choice: a kind word spoken long ago, a fortuitous circumstance, a new relationship, a flash of insight, a memory of love, a sudden opening to faith."[10]

Each recovery story is as unique as its subject. These are, after all, life stories that encompass the entirety of the human experience. However, as we ask what needs to happen for the recovery process to advance, finding answers to one crucial question will prove highly beneficial. It's a question that cuts to the heart of the matter, helping us understand the central elements of the recovery process. In recovery, what are we recovering from? Is it solely the toxic, compulsive relationship with the addictive experience, or is there more to it?

First, we are recovering from the direct relationship with the substance or activity—a relationship that corresponds to changes in habits of thought and action that have become hardwired into the brain. This is the most obvious aspect of the recovery process and involves learning new positive habits of thought and action that make the old ones redundant, a process that inevitably takes time.

An addiction created by a long process of what West and Brown defined as "motivated repetition of the same thoughts and behaviors until they become habitual" cannot be defeated overnight.[11] "Even after you come to hate a drug for ruining your life," writes Adam Alter, "your brain continues to want the drug. It remembers that the drug soothed a psychological need in the past, and so the craving remains. The same is true of behaviors: even as you come to loathe Facebook or Instagram for consuming too much of your time, you continue to want updates as much as you did when they still made you happy."[12] Like driving a car down a dirt road, at first it's exceedingly hard not to follow well-worn tracks, even if you know you'll get into trouble if you do. It takes time, effort, risk—a new wave of "motivated repetition"[13]—to establish new ruts in the road, leading to better destinations.

Brain change cannot be undone with a simple choice to "not pick up" or a one-off action, such as cutting up credit cards or removing dealers' numbers from a phone—vital as such actions can be to kick-start recovery. For old habits to die and new ways of thinking to be established, a new, deep learning process must begin, gain momentum, and reach its goal. The good news—and a source of realistic hope for all in addiction—is that neuroplasticity is never entirely lost, even if it becomes diminished. Marc Lewis writes,

> The brain always retains enough plasticity for new pathways to grow. . . . They may not grow quickly while addicts are first trying to quit, because a tightly focused beam of desire for a well-defined goal has not yet converged. Instead, they are driven by more abstract desires: for freedom, novelty, and lasting contentment. When those goals finally do converge and become concrete . . . new synaptic pathways sprout vigorously again—beyond the well-worn routes that once determined life's narrow boundaries.[14]

Change—as a basic point of neurological *fact*—is always possible. As Gerald May observes, "God creates and cares for us in such a way that our addictions can never completely vanquish our freedom. Addiction may oppress our desire, erode our wills, confound our motivations, and contaminate our judgment, but its bondage is never absolute."[15]

This demanding process is one that often requires assistance from professionals, recovery mentors, and mutual-help groups. At first, recovery may not be possible without withdrawing to a safe environment, such as a residential rehab or the home of a supportive family member, or daily attendance of a support group, like AA or NA. It may involve making significant decisions relating to where we work, friendships and intimate relationships, financial commitments, and social activities—all with the goal of building a life that strengthens our capacity to live life on life's terms, without recourse to the addiction, and minimizing the level of relapse risk to which we are exposed. Recovery will require skill in avoiding and—when there's no alternative—handling "triggers" (people, places, activities, and emotions that, for whatever reason, make us vulnerable to relapse). It may involve a period of Medication-Assisted Treatment (MAT) to "normalize brain chemistry, block the euphoric effects of alcohol and opioids, relieve physiological cravings, and normalize body functions without the negative and euphoric effects of the substance used."[16]

As with most things in recovery, the best approach will likely blend different interventions at different times.

Second, in recovery we are recovering from the impact of underlying issues that make us vulnerable to developing an un-healthy relationship with the object of our addiction. To build a rich and satisfying life in recovery, going beyond simply not picking up or white-knuckling it, we will need to get behind the relationship with substance/activity and address deeper questions. What was it about life in the age of addiction that left the individual searching for the solutions offered by the addictive experience? What stirred the excessive appetite for the rewards provided by weed, wine, or work? What aspects of their habitat and experience mean that "hibernation" makes sense? If the addictive experience was a solution at first, what problem(s) was it solving? What has (or hasn't) happened to leave them hopeless, empty, wounded, and disconnected? "The bottle is not the thing," writes Seth Haines in *Coming Clean*. "The addiction is not the thing. The pain is the thing."[17]

If my painkillers don't work well and have nasty side effects, I can learn strategies to help me break my habit of reaching out for the bottle of pills whenever I feel pain. I can also come to understand better why I'm in pain. Indeed, the process of gaining insight into why addiction found a fertile space in my life can prove to be exceedingly profitable in the recovery process. Something about making sense of things, even if only partially, helps us gain mastery over them. However, explanations are no substitute for solutions. If I can't get to the bottom of my pain and do something about it, I will always be vulnerable to looking to pain pills to help solve my problem. Moreover, even if I can resist the temptation to reach for the bottle, my quality of life remains poor because my pain persists. A healthy recovery, one that grows and bears fruit, has its roots in good soil—in a fertile seedbed for the kind of good life in which addiction serves no good purpose.

THERAPY

How do we turn ground that is rocky, compacted, weedy, and nutrient-poor into a seedbed for growth and flourishing? As we'll see, there is much we can do, but for now, let's focus on two things. Firstly, therapy (counseling, talk therapy, psychotherapy). Most therapy will focus on both the here and now business of the person's relationship with the substance or activity that is the object of addiction and, to a greater or lesser degree, the underlying issues that created a vulnerability to addiction. Therapy may be done one-to-one or in a group setting, with others who share our experiences and are engaged in the recovery process. As with most things in recovery, the best approach will likely blend different interventions at different times according to a highly personalized recipe.

Lucy Foulkes, a lecturer at University College London and author of *Losing Our Minds*, argues that the success of therapy is primarily determined by the quality of the relationship between therapist and client:

> Meta-analyses have found that different types of psychotherapy result in the same level of symptom improvement. . . . Could it be the fact of having therapy, rather than the specifics of therapy itself, is what helps? Proponents of the "common factors" model of psychotherapy believe so and argue that there are a number of features that exist across all successful therapy, which are what drive positive outcomes. One of the key common factors, for example, is the "therapeutic alliance," the working relationship between therapist and patient and, specifically, the quality of their bond and the extent to which their goals for the therapy are aligned. . . . Therapy, when you find the right person, is a strange and wonderful thing. . . . Possibly for the first and only time in your life, you are given the opportunity for your most distressing thoughts or harmful behaviour or darkest fears to be truly heard, without judgement.[18]

In the context of therapeutic work, we need to recognize the additional challenges that the experience of addiction presents for committed Christians. In an interview with *The New Yorker*, Samuel L. Perry, University of Oklahoma sociologist, notes that while conservative

Protestants will, statistically, use pornography "slightly less than your average American," their moral aversion to it adds to the harm it does to them psychologically—a point which may well apply in the case of all addictions: "What I found is that, whatever we think pornography is doing, those effects tend to be amplified when we're talking about conservative Protestants. It seems to be uniquely harmful to conservative Protestants' mental health, their sense of self, their own identities—certainly their intimate relationships—in ways that don't tend to be as harmful for people who don't have that kind of moral problem with it."[19]

RECOVERY CAPITAL

A second means by which we establish a fertile seedbed for recovery is by building up a diverse set of resources labeled *recovery capital.* The concept of recovery capital was developed by Robert Granfield and William Cloud from the University of Denver. Recovery capital refers to "critical elements that an individual possesses, or that exist within his or her immediate surroundings, and that function to promote and sustain a recovery experience."[20] The more recovery capital you have and the more diverse your store of recovery capital is, the more likely your recovery will germinate, take root, mature, and bear fruit.

We can distinguish between four types of recovery capital.[21] The first two (physical and personal capital) are resources that belong to the individual; the second two (social and community capital) are resources that belong to the community.

Physical recovery capital includes the individual's physical and mental health and tangible assets, such as property, transport, and money, that can facilitate recovery (e.g., the capacity to relocate to a safer living context, travel to twelve-step groups, or pay for a detox).

Personal recovery capital includes personal values, vocational skills, education and training, credentials, interpersonal skills, and personal qualities such as self-esteem, self-awareness, self-confidence, problem-solving ability, optimism, and a sense of meaning and purpose.

Social recovery capital refers to the recovery-promoting resources each person has through their relationships, recognizing that people have both support from and obligations to the groups they belong to (for example, family membership provides support but also entails commitments). It may include intimate relationships, family relationships, friendships, and social relationships such as those found at work, school, church, clubs, and twelve-step fellowships.

Finally, community recovery capital refers to recovery-promoting attitudes, policies, and resources within the wider community and culture. It includes

active efforts to reduce addiction/recovery-related stigma, visible and diverse local recovery role models, a full continuum of addiction treatment resources, recovery mutual aid resources that are accessible and diverse, local recovery community support institutions (recovery centers/clubhouses, treatment alumni associations, recovery homes, recovery schools, recovery industries, recovery ministries/churches), and sources of sustained recovery support and early re-intervention (e.g., recovery checkups through treatment programs, employee assistance programs, professional assistance programs, drug courts, or recovery community organizations).[22]

For good reason, the idea of recovery capital has become common currency in the addiction treatment field. It helps us to think very practically about what we can do to strengthen individuals and communities to promote recovery. As we do so, we will come back, again and again, to the primary role of relationships (of all kinds) and community (of all sorts) in the recovery process. As

Bruce Alexander argues in *The Globalization of Addiction*, "The best way out of addiction is overcoming dislocation by finding a secure place in a real community. People sometimes work their way out of dislocation by rejoining their previous worlds of family, friends, and society, with an enhanced appreciation of its importance. Sometimes, however, this familiar world is too fragmented or dysfunctional, and people must create new communities with others who have likewise been forced to build their communities anew."[23]

The individual sits in the driver's seat. None of us can make the choices that lead to freedom for anyone else. However, we cannot overstate the role of relationships in recovery. Recovery happens in community. When it comes to recovery from addiction, as the old Alcoholics Anonymous saying goes, "I can't, but we can." Or, as Huseyin Djemil put it during our Zoom conversation, "no one can do it for you, but you can't do it alone."

ACTIVE INGREDIENT

Toward the end of *The Biology of Desire*, Marc Lewis reflects on a fascinating piece of research conducted by Michael Chandler and colleagues from the University of British Colombia into suicide within Canada's First Nations communities. As they got to know these communities, the first thing that caught the team's attention was the fact that, while the suicide rate among teenagers was at zero in some places and low in many communities, it was staggeringly high in others (five hundred to eight hundred times the national average). "What could possibly make the difference between the places where teens had nothing to live for and those where teens had nothing to die for?" asks Lewis.

Chandler's team set off in search of answers, conducting in-depth interviews with the young people themselves, hoping to make sense of the data. The picture that emerged from their work has profound implications for how we approach addiction recovery and a whole gamut of other issues. "What they found," Lewis writes, "was that young people from the high-suicide communities didn't have stories to tell. . . . They had no clear sense of their past, their childhood, and the generations preceding them. And their attempts to outline possible futures were empty of form and meaning. Unlike the other children, they could not see their lives as narratives, as stories. . . . The kids ate at McDonald's and watched a lot of TV. Their lives were islands clustered in the middle of nowhere. Their lives just didn't make sense. There was only the present, only the featureless terrain of today. . . . They had nothing but the present, nothing to look forward to, so many of them took their own lives."[24]

The addict's life is lived in the tomb of the present.

In the depths of addiction, you exist in the same barren land, consumed with only what is imminent and immediate. "In addiction," writes Lewis, "the relentless preoccupation with immediate rewards carves a small burrow out of the potential richness of time. . . . The fine print tells the story of a tightening spiral of desire, acquisition, and loss, the narrowing of perspective and meaning, the rigid infatuation with reliable, available, but terribly boring rewards— rewards that leave only emptiness and craving in their wake. The addict's life is lived in the tomb of the present."[25] In the dark depths of addiction, there's no horizon to draw you forward, no expectation of dawn's light to lift you out of despair.

Addicts find themselves locked into addiction not only by past pain and present distress but equally by a bleak view of the future that does not allow them to imagine the possibility of being clean and sober.[26] As such, hope is the "active ingredient"—the caffeine in the coffee—of recovery. To hope is both to want something to happen and to believe it is possible. In one of our conversations, Huseyin said something that seems to go against everything we know about addiction. "Stopping was easy," he said. "I was using £200 [$250] a day of heroin and cocaine, but stopping was easy . . . when I had a reason to stop taking drugs. My life had become unmanageable. I was fed up with it. I was seeing more of the problems than the solution. It was making me feel worse and driving me backward. At the point I had a reason to stop, I was fortunate that I had people around me that gave me options."

What made it "easy" for Huseyin to stop using heroin and crack? With the cost of his addiction mounting and benefits diminishing, the first steps of Huseyin's recovery journey felt doable because he both wanted it and, vitally, believed it was possible through the support being offered. In other words, Huseyin found hope—shards of light had broken into the tomb of his present, waking him from hibernation.

REALIGNING DESIRE

To turn first steps into a long-term recovery journey, fresh fuel must be added to the fires of hope. There needs to be a compelling reason to stop the addiction. Someone with decent preexisting reserves of recovery capital, and experience of life outside addiction, will find this much easier than someone without knowledge of life outside addiction and the associated lifestyles of unemployment, homelessness, and crime. Indeed, one person's dreams (like having a family, holding down a job, or owning a car) may be literally beyond another person's imagination—or a source of anxiety—not a reason to stay clean. Nonetheless, finding hope in addiction is essential to finding life in recovery. Success is predicated on a vision for the future that is both desirable and achievable.

"The trick to overcoming addiction," writes Marc Lewis, is "the realignment of desire, so that it switches from the goal of immediate relief to the goal of long-term fulfillment."[27] Stanton Peele makes the same point. "Addicts who begin to replace an addiction with a new relation to the world take a few small steps which are not enough, initially, to guarantee that the new identity can support itself. They are making a leap of faith, starting on a journey whose end point they can only envision at some dim future time. To keep on the path they have laid out they must continually return to the image of the person they ultimately want to be."[28]

Is recovery possible? Absolutely. Is it easy? Not remotely. Recovery is an arduous journey, fraught with danger, that is best not tackled alone. It involves addressing the relationship with the object of the addiction, breaking a habit that has been hardwired into place, and tackling the underlying issues that made the individual vulnerable to the addiction in the first place. For long-term success, recovery capital—physical, personal, social, and community—must be bolstered to deliver the resources needed to operate without the rewards offered by the experience at the heart of their addiction. Animating it all, like yeast kneaded into dough, there must be hope: the desire for recovery, vision for the future, and belief that change is possible.

Chapter 9

BEYOND BATMAN

ROW CHURCH

L A's Skid Row has long been a dark and desperate place where hurting and broken people, drawn from the four corners of America and beyond, huddle together for a fragile sense of safety and community. As Skid Row's population has grown to more than eight thousand people spread across nearly sixty city blocks, the situation has deteriorated. During the summer of 2021, photojournalist Teun Voeten documented life on the streets of Skid Row, producing a series of harrowing photographs that capture the bleak reality of homelessness, active addiction, and untreated mental illness.[1]

Voeten doesn't pull his punches as he describes Skid Row's troubled community.

The rat-infested streets smell of urine and rubbish mixed with the pungent odor of marijuana. Drugs are abundant. . . . Crystal meth, brought in by Mexican cartels and distributed by local gangs in five-dollar bags, is quickly overtaking crack as the drug of choice. Substance abuse used to be a discreet activity: people drank super-strength beers hidden in paper brown bags. Now they smoke meth and crack in the open in glass pipes. In front of the needle exchange on Fifth Street, people inject speedballs, a mixture of heroin and crystal meth, right on the pavement. Mental illness is rife, and half-naked people scream, talk to the air and defecate in the middle of the streets.[2]

Skid Row is a place that seems entirely lost to the darkness, to spiritual forces that "steal and kill and destroy" (John 10:10), but Pastor Cue, the founder and pastor of Row Church, doesn't see it that way. "It's the homeless capital of America, but believe it or not," Cue says, "Skid Row is a place where people come to find hope. After Skid Row, you have nothing left. There ain't but one way to go, and that's up. Most of the people on Skid Row are on the way up."[3]

Row Church is a church, quite literally, without walls. Every Friday night, Pastor Cue and his flock gather right at the heart of the darkness that engulfs Skid Row. They meet to worship, hear God's Word, pray for one another, fellowship over a hot meal, and provide practical assistance to those living their lives on Skid Row's sidewalks. The Row Church has no building, not because it can't afford one, but because it doesn't want one. Row Church's sanctuary is the street. "We hold service outdoors, under the beautiful night's sky. As a church without walls, our services take place on an active street corner, surrounded by the sounds of sirens, cars, and various chatter. It is in this very environment that we see the Word of God go forth and capture the hearts of men and women, even in the midst of chaos and distractions."[4]

When Pastor Cue looks at the parish he's served for close to two decades, he sees things that few others do. He looks beyond the squalid streets, tattered tents, disturbed minds, and hustling hands—and into the eyes of the people. He knows their names and their stories. He perceives their potential and conceives of practical solutions that could unlock it. He recognizes "the least of these" (Matt. 25:40), and in them, Jesus and the chance to serve Him. Moreover, he sees signs of God at work. "I love this place!" he says. "You wanna know why? Because God is alive on this block, you hear me? He is alive. Here, we say the gospel is airborne; you never know where it's going to land. It just takes off. It's all about loving people and loving them without strings—and God will pull on the strings of their hearts."[5]

I visited Row Church on a cold Friday evening in February of 2020, a few short weeks before the COVID-19 pandemic turned the world upside down. In preparation, I spent the afternoon exploring the streets of Skid Row. I wanted to get a sense of what it would be like to call this place *home*. I was struck by the constant movement of LAPD patrols—around and around they went, seemingly stuck on repeat—and by the way groups of people gathered around music, a different sound on every street, and oil-drum fires that were lit as night fell. Even on Skid Row's haunted streets, there is friendship and community. Indeed, these tents provide more than shelter. They are homes, dwellings around which makeshift families do life together.

Early in the evening, Pastor Cue and his team of volunteers arrived to begin setting up for church, just like they always do, and as their music started to play, their community slowly gathered. The service proceeded as most do—welcome, worship, preach, prayer—before a meal was served. Some who gathered

Amid darkness, despair, and agitation, these are people of peace creating a place of light and hope.

were regulars; others were newcomers, some just to the church, others to the neighborhood of Skid Row. Pastor Cue's sermon was from Paul's letter to Philemon. It was a message of hope: a declaration of the gospel's power to transform us from "slaves" into "sons" and "brothers" in the family of God.

As the meal was served, I stepped away from the church and crossed the street to a spot where I could look across at the Row Church family eating and talking together. Amid darkness, despair, and agitation, these are people of peace creating a place of light and hope. That hope was expressed in many things: a warm welcome, a kind word, practical help, and the call to follow Jesus. It is, however, rooted in one thing—the gospel of Jesus Christ.

BATMAN & SPIDER-MAN

Whenever I talk about addiction recovery, it's never long before I find myself talking about superheroes, specifically an important distinction between how Batman and Spider-Man accomplish their feats. It's a crude illustration but one that helps us as we think about the gospel and the process of long-term recovery.[6]

According to those concerned with such matters, Batman isn't a true superhero. Instead, because he lacks superpowers, Bruce Wayne, the Caped Crusader, is classified as no more than a "costumed crime-fighter." Batman does what Batman does because he's learned the right skills, developed the right attitudes, cultivated the right relationships, and mastered the right tools for the job. Batman's capacity to fight crime is related to a set of resources, internal and external, which he has developed with time, energy, and practice. Spider-Man's crime-fighting capacity is rooted in something different. You know the story. Peter Parker, a twisted-up American teenager, struggling with feelings of rejection and inadequacy, gets bitten by a radioactive spider during a school science experiment. That bite triggered something that transformed Peter Parker into Spider-Man from the inside out.

In the previous chapter, we explored the process of addiction recovery. As we did so, we touched on the role of support groups, therapy, recovery capital, relapse-prevention planning, rehab, medication, and more. This is the Batman-stuff of recovery, and it's vital to long-term success in the daily battle against the destructive habits of thought and action we call *addiction*.

As the church, we have a powerful role to play in helping those engaged in the fight against addiction. We can do this in a multitude of ways, many of which involve little or no specialized training or experience. Simply being the kind, genuine, accepting, prayerful community God calls us to be, we will be a source of much-needed recovery capital, and even more so as we develop initiatives—like counseling services and supported housing programs—designed to promote recovery.

As God's people, we must go beyond Batman. In the age of addiction, the heart of our calling is the call to proclaim the good news that through Jesus Christ, we can have a living relationship with the God—Father, Son, and Holy Spirit—who transforms us, like Spider-Man, from the inside out. This gospel isn't *just* good news about personal transformation. It's good news about a work of divine universal re-creation, into which personal human transformation is just one, albeit central, element. Theologian N. T. Wright puts it like this: "The God who made the world, with all its parts and pieces, is now active in remaking it, restoring it, healing it, and renewing it; and the means by which he has done the first and is doing the second is the person, the man, we know as Jesus Christ."[7] This gospel is good news for the world that we have described in the first section of this book—a world so hostile to human well-being that vast numbers of us hibernate in addictive experiences. Moreover, and more immediately, it's good news for anyone trying to wake up from the survival-sleep of addiction, for God has chosen to begin this work of universal re-creation with human beings, specifically people, who like those brought low by addiction, are "poor in spirit" (Matt. 5:3–4).

SONS, NOT SLAVES

"I stink. You don't want to hug me." Neil and I stood at the bottom of Yeldall Manor's driveway, its majestic avenue of giant redwoods towering above us. Driving to work early one morning, I'd noticed movement in the bushes and had stopped to investigate. Soon enough, Neil emerged. I knew Neil well from his first time on the program the year before. Initially, he stayed sober, but a Christmas slipup led to months spent in and out of the hospital and sleeping rough in garages and sheds. Now, desperate for help, Neil was camped out in the shrubbery at the bottom of the drive.

It was too late to abort the hug. I don't remember a smell. I just remember a good man who desperately needed to know he was loved and accepted—just as he was. His words communicated more than a need for a hot shower and some fresh clothes. They expressed the shame of a man, brought to his knees by addiction, whose sense of self-worth was shot to pieces. In his own words, he was "broken, beaten, and with nothing left of self or material things."[8]

Jesus' story of the Lost Son, which climaxes with the most famous embrace in history, must surely be among the most relatable of the parables. Though set in a culture with customs very different from our own, it's not hard to imagine the same drama playing out on our doorsteps.

"A man had two sons. The younger son told his father, 'I want my share of your estate now before you die.' So his father agreed to divide his wealth between his sons.

"A few days later, this younger son packed all his belongings and moved to a distant land, and there he wasted all his money in wild living. About the time his money ran out, a great famine swept over the land, and he began to starve. He persuaded a local farmer to hire him, and the man sent him into his fields to feed the pigs. The young man became so hungry that even the pods he was feeding the pigs looked good to him. But no one gave him anything." (Luke 15:11–16 NLT)

Nothing in the text directly indicates that the Lost Son was addicted to the experiences that Jesus calls "wild living." Nevertheless, like addiction, this lifestyle was expensive, rapidly consuming the son's inheritance, and absorbed him so thoroughly that he only stopped once the money ran out. However, the precise nature of the son's experience is not the parable's primary concern. Nor should it be ours. Instead, Jesus' focus is on the radical actions of the father.

"When he finally came to his senses, he said to himself, 'At home, even the hired servants have food enough to spare, and here I am dying of hunger! I will go home to my father and say, "Father, I have sinned against both heaven and you, and I am no longer worthy of being called your son. Please take me on as a hired servant.'"

"So he returned home to his father. And while he was still a long way off, his father saw him coming. Filled with love and compassion, he ran to his son, he embraced him, and kissed him. His son said to him, 'Father, I have sinned against both heaven and you, and I am no longer worthy of being called your son.'

"But his father said to the servants, 'Quick! Bring the finest robe in the house and put it on him. Get a ring for his finger and sandals for his feet. And kill the calf we have been fattening. We must celebrate with a feast, for this son of mine was dead and has now returned to life. He was lost, but now he is found.' So the party began." (Luke 15:17–24 NLT)

New Testament scholar Kenneth Bailey spent forty years teaching theology in the Middle East. Among his many influential works, *Poet & Peasant* casts light on several details of the parable, easily hidden from modern Western eyes, that help us understand the radical nature of Jesus' portrayal of the father heart of God. He highlights the very public nature of the encounter and the father's protectiveness toward a son vulnerable to a village's anger.

What the father does in this homecoming scene can best be understood as a series of dramatic actions calculated to protect the boy from the hostility of the village and to restore him to fellowship in the community. These actions begin with the father running down the road. An Oriental nobleman with flowing robes never runs anywhere. To do so is humiliating. . . . The father makes the reconciliation public at the edge of the village. His son enters the village under the protective care of his father's acceptance.[9]

Next, Bailey directs our attention to the father's lavish outpouring of love and grace that sees the son, a slave to sin, enter not by the back door to take the place of a servant but celebrated as a son before the whole community.

Rather than experiencing the ruthless hostility he deserves and anticipates, the son witnesses an unexpected, visible demonstration of love. . . . There are no words of acceptance and welcome. The love expressed is too profound for words. . . . The servants are told to dress the son as servants do a king. He is not told to go and bathe and change his clothes. . . . The best robe is most certainly the father's. . . . The ring is quite likely a signet ring, which means that he is trusted in a remarkable way. The shoes are a sign of being a free man in the house, not a servant. . . . The selection of a goat or a sheep means that most, if not all, the village will be present that evening. . . . The calf means a joy so great that it must be celebrated with the grandest banquet imaginable.[10]

In truth, the Lost Son is a story that could never have happened in "real life." No first-century Jewish father in his right mind would have behaved this way. This, then, is an extraordinary story, shocking and disruptive, told to demonstrate the exceptional qualities of the God about whom King David sings:[11]

> Praise the LORD, my soul,
>   and forget not all his benefits—
> who forgives all your sins
>   and heals all your diseases,
> who redeems your life from the pit
>   and crowns you with love and compassion,
> who satisfies your desires with good things
>   so that your youth is renewed like the eagle's. . . .
> The LORD is compassionate and gracious,
>   slow to anger, abounding in love.
> (Ps. 103:2–5, 8)

Where the world rejects and withholds, the Father welcomes and protects. Where the world writes off, the Father never gives up. Where the world pulls away—often with good reason—the Father draws us close. As His robes settle on our shoulders, He restores our identity. We are sons and daughters, not slaves. He brings us into His household, into the sphere of His rule. Here we are protected.

The Father sees us, runs toward us, and buries our sin and shame in His embrace.

Peace reigns. We enjoy the fellowship of family. As He places a ring on our finger, He dignifies us with the responsibility of ruling and marks us as His heirs. As He calls for the fattened calf, He signals that we now live within the realm of His provision. This is the startling message of the story of the Lost Son for those who, broken down, beaten up, and emptied out by the baffling mix of volition and coercion that characterizes addiction, have turned toward home. The gospel of Jesus Christ is the good news that, whether our idol is a solution in a syringe, odds on a screen, the curves of the human body, or anything else in God's creation, the Father sees us, runs toward us, and buries our sin and shame in His embrace.

My encounter with Neil on the Yeldall driveway took place in the spring of 2011. "I was completely broken," Neil recalls. "I'd prayed that either God would take my life or open the door to Yeldall. He chose the latter." More than a decade later, as I prepare the final draft of this book, Neil shared a personal update with Yeldall's ex-residents:

This weekend is a bit of a milestone for me. In March 2012, I left Yeldall after completing the program. The 3rd of May is my 10th wedding anniversary, so a double celebration! Has it been easy? No. Have I always made the best choices? No. Have I made mistakes? Plenty. Has God been faithful? Yes. Has He led and guided me? Yes. God willing, in July this year, I will complete my training as a Baptist minister. There have been times of tremendous joy and times of grief and sadness. Times of being built-up and times of tearing down. Throughout, Jesus has been a constant companion. He redeemed me from a pit I put myself in. I am 11 years sober and following Him the best way I can. My testimony is that God, by grace, through Jesus, saves the sheep that strayed.[12]

EASY WAY

Despite growing up in a stable, well-off family in a nice middle-class area of the Midlands of England, my friend Keith found himself chained to a bottle for over twenty years, losing jobs, partners, and his children as a result. Why did Keith drink? What made him vulnerable to addiction? "I didn't feel like I belonged anywhere; I didn't feel like anyone loved me. The only way I could gain any feeling of goodness was when I discovered alcohol at eleven. Mum and Dad were out at work, so I just helped myself to the drinks cabinet."

It took time for Keith's drinking to seize control. He graduated from school with good grades and secured a decent job with the Ministry of Defence, starting him off on a career that would help sustain his first love: his relationship with alcohol. "I earned good money, but the more I got, the more it just fueled my addiction. I was a mess. I didn't care about anybody. The only person I cared about was me and where my next fix was coming from." As the years went by, the pace of his drinking and drug-taking escalated. Unable to hold down a job and with no income, he found himself homeless on Leicester's streets. Those hard streets would prove Keith's rock bottom, the solid foundation on which his recovery is built.

Keith's first glimmers of hope came through the work of a Christian outreach team and a powerful encounter with God.

> I never had any sort of Christian upbringing at all. I did believe there was a God, but that was all. But while I was on the streets, there was a Christian team who came round feeding the homeless. I liked them, and I started thinking that maybe there was something in this Christian thing after all.

One morning, I was in a squat (abandoned building), needles and bottles all around me. It had been raining heavily. A shaft of light came through this broken window, and I felt that God was speaking to me. I audibly heard Him say, "You've got to follow this light, you've got to follow me, and you've got to pick up your mat and walk." The next day, I went to the Alcohol Advice Centre and told them I needed help—not detox but rehab, a Christian rehab.[13]

Looking back on his recovery journey, this is Keith's encouragement to others: "Love Jesus, because He will guide you all the way, and He will see you through to the other side. There is a better life, trust me."

In the age of addiction, what is Jesus' message? To those who despair, suffocating for lack of hope, Jesus says, "The thief comes only to steal and kill and destroy; I have come that [you] may have life, and have it to the full" (John 10:10). To those who feel empty, who hunger for true satisfaction, Jesus says, "I am the bread of life. Whoever comes to me will never go hungry, and whoever believes in me will never be thirsty" (John 6:35). To those wounded by the world, perhaps by people who should have kept them safe, Jesus draws us closer to the God who "heals the brokenhearted and binds up their wounds" (Ps. 147:3). To those whose lives lack meaning and purpose, Jesus says, "Go and make disciples of all nations, baptizing them in the name of the Father and of the Son and of the Holy Spirit" (Matt. 28:19). To those isolated, who feel alone, Jesus says, "Surely I am with you always, to the very end of the age" (Matt. 28:20).

How do we access all of this? Simply by responding to Christ's call to follow Him. It's the same call He issued to His first disciples, which has transformed countless lives down the ages, and which captivated Keith's heart in that Leicester squat. "Come to me, all you who are weary and burdened, and I will give you rest. Take my yoke upon you and learn from me, for I am gentle and humble in heart, and you will find rest for your souls. For my yoke is easy and my burden is light" (Matt. 11:28–30).

Like all first-century Jewish rabbis, Jesus had a "yoke." A yoke was a rabbi's way of reading Scripture and, as they applied it to life, their wider teaching on how to live well as God's children and experience the *shalom* of His kingdom. Yokes tended to be hard. Jesus' yoke was His way of living. It was, John Mark Comer writes, "His way to shoulder the (at times crippling) weight of life—marriage, divorce, prayer, money, sex, conflict resolution, government—all of it."[14] And, the most startling thing about Jesus' yoke was that it was *easy*, not hard. Jesus' call was to a new way characterized by *freedom*. Eugene Peterson paraphrases Jesus' words like this: "Walk with me and work with me—watch how I do it. Learn the unforced rhythms of grace. I won't lay anything heavy or ill-fitting on you. Keep company with me and you'll learn to live freely and lightly" (Matt. 11:28–30 MSG).

"Freedom," writes theologian Stanley Hauerwas, "is not some kind of freedom of choice but rather a calling into a way of life that frees us from being determined by our desires."[15] Isn't this precisely the life sought by all in recovery—a life in which they can exercise control over their previously overpowering desire for the object of their addiction? It's a way of life we discover as, one day at a time, we take up the yoke that keeps us close to Jesus, right where we can see Him working, hear His voice, and sense His presence. It's the way of life Jesus taught in the Sermon on the Mount and lived out in the Gospels. It's the way practiced by the first disciples in all that we read about in Acts and the New Testament letters. Jesus' way or yoke is a lifestyle, not just "a set of ideas (what we call theology) or a list of dos and don'ts (what we call ethics)."[16] It's a way of life shaped by Scripture, empowered by the Spirit, shared in community, and structured around a set of habits we call spiritual disciplines or practices.

"Why do you think there's so much addiction in our world?" asks

John Mark Comer. "Not just substance abuse but the more run-of-the-mill addictions to porn or sex or eating or dieting or exercise or work or travel or shopping or social media or even church?" His answer?

> People all over the world—outside the church and in—are looking for an escape, a way out from under the crushing weight to life this side of Eden. But there is no escaping it. The best the world can offer is a temporary distraction to delay the inevitable or deny the inescapable. That's why Jesus doesn't offer us an escape. He offers us something far better: "equipment." He offers his apprentices a whole new way to bear the weight of our humanity: with ease. At his side. Like two oxen in a field, tied shoulder to shoulder. With Jesus doing all the heavy lifting. At his pace. Slow, unhurried, present to the moment, full of love and joy and peace. An easy life isn't an option; an easy yoke is.[17]

INSTEAD

In the face of the destructive power of addiction, the gospel is the good news that we are transformed from slaves into sons and daughters as we turn to Christ. As we then follow Him, seeking to live life His way, we discover living hope, deep satisfaction, healing and wholeness, and supportive community. But that's not everything. Summarizing the gospel for the Galatian church, Paul wrote:

> God sent his Son, born of a woman, born under the law, to redeem those under the law, that we might receive adoption to sonship. Because you are his sons, God sent the Spirit of his Son into our hearts, the Spirit who calls out, "Abba, Father." So you are no longer a slave, but God's child; and since you are his child, God has made you also an heir. (Gal. 4:4–7)

The promise of the gift of the Holy Spirit is essential to the gospel. Our experience of both sonship and discipleship is contingent on the Holy Spirit's work within us. Through the Spirit, God meets those deep needs that, left unsatisfied, make us vulnerable to developing toxic relationships with the objects of addiction.

Jesus stood and said in a loud voice, "Let anyone who is thirsty come to me and drink. Whoever believes in me, as Scripture has said, rivers of living water will flow from within them." By this he meant the Spirit, whom those who believed in him were later to receive. (John 7:37–39)

"Where the Spirit of the Lord is," Paul declared, "there is freedom" (2 Cor. 3:17). This liberty is not an abstract state. It is the by-product of a life lived "in step with the Spirit" (Gal. 5:25), whose presence, according to the New Testament writers, results in peace of mind (Rom. 8:16), wisdom and insight (Eph. 1:17), unity in relationships (Eph. 2:22), inner strength (Eph. 3:16), victory over temptation (Gal. 5:16), and an abundance of the life-giving qualities we call the "fruit of the Spirit"— love, joy, peace, patience, kindness, goodness, faithfulness, gentleness, and self-control (Eph. 5:22–23).

> Addictions take root because a potentially addictive experience meets legitimate and felt needs, at least for a time.

In this context, and given the rewards that addictive experiences offer, Paul delivers a provocative challenge to the Ephesians. "Do not get drunk on wine," he tells them. "Instead, be filled with the Spirit, speaking to one another with psalms, hymns, and songs from the Spirit" (Eph. 5:18–19). Addictions take root because a potentially addictive experience, like getting "drunk on wine," meets legitimate and felt needs, at least for a time. In contrast, the Spirit—and the fellowship with God's people we find in the Spirit—cultivates relationships through which our deepest longings may be truly satisfied.

SOMETHING BETTER

Huseyin, whom we met in the previous chapter, is clear that when drugs came into his life, they delivered something far more valuable to him than just a "buzz" or a "high."

"I've been traumatized, I've gone through parents divorcing, Dad killing someone, Dad going to prison, violence in the home, a whole incongruence between the culture at home and the culture of my community as a Turkish kid growing up in North London," he tells me. "Through all of that, I couldn't run away. I couldn't fight back—I was a little kid. I couldn't ask for help as much as I would have liked. When I found drugs and, to some degree, crime, it really helped me. When I first took heroin, I remember thinking, *Why isn't everyone doing this? This is the best thing since sliced bread.* The drugs made a difference, not just to how I felt. They connected me back to myself. They connected me to others, and they connected me to the world around me. Drug use was an answer to the way I was feeling. It was a solution, my first attempt at healing. I discovered something that worked, and it was fast-acting, so I grabbed it with both hands."

Long before it's a problem, addiction is a solution. In drugs, Huseyin found a way to satisfy genuine and legitimate needs. In recovery, those same underlying problems, plus the additional issues resulting from life in addiction still need a solution. At Yeldall Manor, in the early days of his recovery, Huseyin discovered just that. "If I'm using drugs and drugs work, for me to stop using drugs, I've got to find something better, something that works. When I found recovery in the form of Christianity, in the form of a relationship with Jesus, in the form of mentoring relationships with people who gave me something of themselves, it was a better solution. Comparing the solution that I found in God, in Jesus Christ, in a personal relationship, to all the other things that I've tried and might try, it stands the test of time. It's the strongest; it holds the most water; it's the kindest to me. I've found something that works."

To the person enslaved by elements of their own self, to desires and habits that have taken on a life of their own, the gospel is the good news that the living God can transform them from the inside out (2 Cor. 5:17). To the person who feels ashamed, empty, and alone, it's the good news that the living God can free them with His pardon, soothe them with His peace, and animate them with His joy. To the person who feels impotent and powerless, it is the good news that the living God wants to fill them with His Spirit, to fortify them with His strength. To the person who feels isolated—maybe even utterly abandoned—it's the good news that there is a people among whom His presence rests. To the person who tragically ends their life still in the grip of addiction, it's the good news that though addiction may have won in this life, the victory of Christ guarantees total freedom in the life to come.

Chapter 10

RAT PARK CHURCH

TRANSFORMATIONAL COMMUNITY

The whole lifestyle went way out of control—the party was over in 2008 but didn't end until 2014." My friend Tom, who we met earlier, got sober in early 2014 after what he describes, with no sense of exaggeration, as a "year from hell" that encompassed drug-induced psychosis, obsessive suicidal thoughts, septum-repair surgery, and unrelenting anxiety.

In the middle of that brutal year, Tom had a powerful spiritual experience that would prove to be a watershed in his story. "My God encounter moment happened sometime in the fall of 2013, I don't remember exactly when," he explains during a conversation in my office at Novō's center in Santa Cruz, Bolivia. "I had spent the entire summer just gorging myself with drugs and going from club to music festival to bar around New York. I was sitting in my mom's living room one day, and I was just overwhelmed with an immediate sense of lucidity and peace. I had been under constant mental and emotional torment for months. I had been trying to take more and more drugs to suppress it, but it was only making it worse. I don't remember what I was thinking about at the time or if I prayed. Still, in an instant, I went from months of drug-induced fog and hallucinations to complete mental clarity, just like everything became very stable and still all of a sudden."

Tom tells me how he felt drawn to his mom's bookshelf, where he picked up a copy of *The Big Book*. "I opened the book and started reading about an experience Bill Wilson, founder of AA, had in a hospital room that was so close to the experience I was having at that moment. I had a clear and immediate sense of God's presence and that He was speaking to me. I had a very intense conviction in that moment to reach out for help. I immediately called a psychiatrist I had been assigned to see while on probation years before."

Although powerfully impacted by that experience, Tom's recovery wouldn't begin until an encounter after class on February 13, 2014. "I'm sitting in an introduction to psychology class, where I had to introduce myself. I'm all hopped-up on drugs, looking like a mess. The one guy on campus who's in AA is in the room. I'd seen him around but didn't know who he was and that he was sober. After the class, he came up to me, gave me a cigarette, and asked me, 'Hey, can you stay sober tonight?' and I was like, 'I'll try.' He invited me to his dorm, where he shared his whole story with me. He brought me to a meeting the next night, and when I walked into the meeting, the girl sitting up at the table was one of my best friends. She's someone I used to do all the drinking and partying with. She burst into tears, 'I've been praying for you for like three years because we all thought you were going to die.' I had no idea she was sober."

In the early days of his addiction, relationships were every bit a part of the "solution" offered by the lifestyle, as were the drugs themselves. In a group of friends exploring the world of sex, drugs, and hip-hop together, Tom found a sense of identity, family, and new community, having disconnected from a family in whom he'd lost trust. But, just as his addiction was forged in community, so too was his recovery. Since 2014, in a group of friends exploring the world of recovery and faith together, Tom has discovered a transformational community.

At first, Alcoholics Anonymous was a crucial source of accountability and recovery-affirming relationships. Then, after moving to California to pursue a relationship that soon fell through, he connected with church for the first time. "I ended up in an AA, and this Christian AA guy wandered up and invited me to church. The second I got there, they matched me up with an older guy, Jeff, a mentor of mine. They had a Celebrate Recovery group I was doing for a couple of years. Nic, the missions pastor, took me under his wing to disciple me."

"My entire life has changed," Tom tells me. "I've had incredible encounters with God. I've jumped deeply into missions, charismatic movements, service, and prayer. I am in leadership in my church, host Bible studies and prayer groups in my home, and am deeply rooted in service of the Christian community. I've committed myself to leading friends and family to the Lord, watching many around me come to faith from childhood, my AA community, college friends, and family members."

> How do we ensure that our churches are characterized by hope, satisfaction, wholeness, and connection?

As God's people, imperfect communities in diverse contexts, what can we do to help prevent addiction in our community? How do we help those in active addiction, who, like Tom, are fighting for their lives? How do we ensure that our churches are characterized by hope, satisfaction, wholeness, and connection—qualities that are in such short supply in the age of addiction? How do we become communities that are less Skinner box and more Rat Park?

There are, of course, no simple one-size-fits-all answers to these questions. Each local church community must formulate the specifics of its responses. So, too, must nonprofits, outreach ministries, treatment centers, and others. Our responses will be shaped by the particulars of our theology, churchmanship, demographic, culture, history, and corporate "personality," as well as a desire to complement the work that others in the wider community are already doing. As such, I have avoided recommendations relating to specific recovery-focused initiatives (e.g., setting up a Celebrate Recovery group or establishing a sober house). The suggestions below are inclusive and, in the best sense, generic. They can be applied in a broad range of contexts and, where adopted, they will engage the whole church community.

DEPTH

So, what can we do to become addiction-preventing, recovery-promoting communities? First, and perhaps most important, we can pursue greater depth in our relationship with God—Father, Son, and Holy Spirit. The age of addiction needs church communities that go deeper. A Christian life characterized by event attendance, superficial relationships, performance, discipleship-as-intellectual-exercise, feel-good sermons, easy answers, and low expectations might work quite nicely for some. For the addict, in a life-and-death battle to stay sober, "just for today," knowing their next fix is just a WhatsApp message away, it won't cut it.

Emerging from an all-consuming reward-delivering relationship with booze, betting, or masturbation, addicts in recovery need an intimate personal relationship with the living God and a true spiritual home amongst others who also know Him. It's what we all need. We need a sense of His abiding and active presence in our lives. Daily, we need to hear God's voice, feel His love, and experience His peace, comfort, grace, and mercy. We need access to the Spirit's counsel and strength. We need to see that same Spirit bear fruit in our lives. We need the *shalom* that an abundance of love, joy, peace, patience, kindness, goodness, faithfulness, gentleness, and self-control brings to our lives and relationships (Gal. 5:22–23).

Being God-adjacent isn't enough. Our churches must be God-connected communities that lead us all into a vital, genuine, life-giving relationship with Him. "Addiction," writes Aaron White,

> gives us a temporary escape from our feelings and a deadening of our senses, but it is only a pale substitute for life in all its fullness because none of these surrogates ultimately satisfy. . . . We are invested with a profound longing for fulfillment, for wholeness, for kinship, and for love—longings that can only be satisfied by something outside of ourselves. This necessarily includes human community. . . . But even human community is not enough. We were created with an inner desire for God, a deep yearning for relationship with our Creator, a relationship that contains within it our very meaning and purpose. Knowing and pursuing our heart's divine longing is central to finding our way—and helping others to find their way—out of addiction and into recovery.[1]

HABITS

The second thing the church can do is place the practice of the spiritual habits at the heart of our life together. These habits—often known as *disciplines* or *practices*—include silence, solitude, sabbath, simplicity, fasting, and a daily pattern of prayer that includes worship, confession, and meditation on Scripture. "The disciplines,"

Dallas Willard explains, "are activities of mind and body purposefully undertaken, to bring our personality and total being into effective cooperation with the divine order. They enable us more and more to live in a power that is, strictly speaking, beyond us, deriving from the spiritual realm itself."[2]

Life in addiction is so immersive, focused, and consistent. It follows familiar, comforting pathways through each day. It pivots around particular objects and actions. The spiritual disciplines provide us with a new set of habits and patterns around which to build daily life. They give a concrete focus to the development of our relationship with God. For those on the path out of addiction, the spiritual habits will function as a kind of trellis around which they can grow and experience the kind of rich, dynamic, satisfying relationship with God that precludes the need for what our addictive relationships have given us. A focus on the habits shared by a congregation or small group can also provide a common architecture to spiritual life that can deepen our relationships with one another. For others, establishing these life-giving habits will prevent us from developing unhealthy relationships with the substance or activity that appears to offer the best solution to our problems.

Instinctively, we may recoil from anything that looks like "asking too much" of someone in early recovery. And yet, though it may be counterintuitive to many of us, structures, expectations, responsibility, and service provide a much-needed sense of purpose and meaning to each day in early recovery. Maybe we need to ask more?

VILLAGE

In his recovery memoir, *Coming Clean*, attorney Seth Haines attributes his ability to find lasting freedom from his addiction to alcohol to the support he found in his church community. "My friends in Austin taught me it takes a village to break through to freedom.

These cycles of addiction (no matter the addiction), the breaking of them—it's tricky business. When I'm sober-minded, anxiety lurks, doubts nag, and the ghosts beckon. When I'm sober-minded, the contours of life are more angular, the textures rougher. . . . When I'm sober-minded, though, I hear the wisdom of my community and can lean on its strength. I can muster the courage to drink water or call my wife or be honest about my dependency. When I'm sober-minded, I can also hear the truth of the Spirit—I am a self-medicator; this moment is painful; self-medicating with alcohol squeezes the still small voice from the mind. When I'm sober-minded, Scripture comes alive."[3]

> The church we need is a community in which we see every person's gifts expressed.

How do we become communities that are crucibles of spiritual, emotional, relational, and physical flourishing in a world of addiction? Third, by pursuing richer relationships with one another. When so many feel isolated and disconnected, God's people need to pull together, moving closer and going deeper. Not just for the sake of those, like Tom and Seth, walking the path, both steep and narrow, of recovery from addiction. But also as a means of "addiction-proofing" ourselves and, particularly, our young people.

The kind of close community we need will involve more than simply developing a few close, intimate connections with people with whom we naturally resonate. The community we need is more diverse than that. Of course, we all need the kinds of close friendships that feel "easy" and life-giving, but we also need a "twelve" who will help us grow and a "seventy-two" with whom we can serve and look outwards (Matt. 5–7; Luke 10:1–23). We need spiritual brothers and sisters. We need spiritual parents and grandparents. We need the help of "experts" and "specialists" who can strengthen us to face specific challenges. The church we need is a community in which we see every person's gifts expressed. It's a body whose every part is vital to the well-being of the whole.

In this context, Seth Haines's language of *village* is helpful. A village is a multigenerational, potentially multicultural, community of people who share a sense of history, purpose, and identity. It's a diverse network of interdependent relationships that helps everyone flourish. Surely, this is precisely the kind of community each of us—addicted or not—needs to protect and sustain us through the inclemency of life in the modern world.

As we seek to develop richer relationships, and to walk with those battling addiction, perhaps we need to create spaces where members of our church community can gather daily. "Ninety meetings in ninety days!" is often the first suggestion a newcomer to AA or any of the other twelve-step fellowships will hear. Some go further, asking: "If you're not at work, or volunteering, or helping out your family, why aren't you at a meeting?" The idea is simple: as you start out in recovery, you need the fellowship of others in your community—and the strength, encouragement, and wisdom it provides—every day, not just some days. As churches, perhaps there's something for us to learn here. How would our communities look if there were daily opportunities for those who want to gather—perhaps over a simple meal or coffee—just to be together? The idea isn't that everyone meets every day. Rather, it's that some people gather every day so that everyone knows they have a place and people where they will find friendship and support, prayer, and wisdom. Such a space could play a critical role for those dealing with addictions as a complement to mutual-aid groups such as AA and Celebrate Recovery. It could also prove to be a preventative intervention for those vulnerable to developing addictions and a source of blessing to those who are new to faith, who feel isolated and lonely, or who are struggling with mental health or other personal issues.

CHAMPIONS

To become transformational communities in an age of addiction, the fourth thing we can do is give space at the very core of our churches to those with experience of addiction and recovery. For too long, addiction has been confined to the margins. We need to hear from those who have wrestled with addiction. We need their leadership. That doesn't mean placing those in recovery on pedestals that stop them from sharing their struggles honestly, setting them up on the kinds of pedestals that set them up for a fall. It means encouraging their influence on our worship services, discipleship groups, outreach projects, social activities, and more.

Aaron White, National Director of 24-7 Prayer Canada and author of *Recovering*, lives and works in Vancouver's Downtown Eastside. He speaks to the powerful dynamic that develops when those in recovery move from the fringes to the center of Christian communities:

> Many of the men and women I know in recovery are . . . doing the hard work of soul discovery and mind renewal in ways that make them seem more like monks than drunks. As a result, they have grasped hold of spiritual blessings that I have rarely seen in the church. But they need help. They need more than just a spiritual awakening. They need communities that can receive and support them and believe with them in the possibility of transformation. They need communities that know a Higher Power by name and have experienced his liberation. They need communities that are willing to admit they need help. . . . And the church needs the blessing brought by these spiritual pilgrims-in-recovery as well. There is nothing more challenging and life-giving than an infusion of people who have walked a hard road, confessed to weaknesses

and faults, and found deliverance and hope. This kind of vulnerability and honesty can provoke godly sorrow and repentance among the rest of us comfortable addicts. It can make us take seriously the life-altering promises of our faith and the attachments that are keeping us from accessing those blessings.[5]

In our commitment to bringing addiction and recovery in from the margins, we should consider appointing a recovery "champion," making them visible and empowering them to shape and strengthen our churches. What a recovery champion will do will vary according to their gifts and the nature of the church. A recovery champion may act as a point person charged with integrating newcomers in addiction and recovery. They may facilitate training for leaders and volunteers to help them support those in recovery. They may run recovery-focused small groups, lead recovery-focused service programs in the local community, and provide pastoral support to members dealing with addiction within their families. They may connect the church with other services and organizations within the wider community, such as twelve-step fellowships, counseling services, day programs, and rehabs. Recovery champions may help guide the whole church community as it reflects on difficult questions, such as how we relate to alcohol in social settings or how to best support a member who has relapsed.

RETHINKING GROUPS

An academic philosopher's study is, perhaps, an unlikely place to go in search of insight into the down-to-earth business of addiction recovery. Indeed, walking around the relaxed campus of Biola University, I feel far from the distressed lives I encountered in Skid Row, just miles away. And yet, as I talk with Kent Dunnington, author of *Addiction and Virtue: Beyond the Models of Disease and Choice*, I discover a rich source of practical wisdom.

Kent's interest in addiction has its roots in his experience of what he, a nonalcoholic master's student at Texas A&M University, experienced in the meeting rooms of Alcoholics Anonymous. "I was sort of casting about," Kent tells me. "It was a really dark period for me, and the person who ended up being my mentor was this guy named John McDermott. He was a classical American philosopher and a lapsed Catholic who, nevertheless, was really on about the spiritual life. And he was a recovering alcoholic. For him, AA had become a deeply spiritual way of life, even though he considered himself agnostic. I think partly because I was just depressed, he said, 'You should come with me to AA.' So, I did. That was my initial introduction to addiction and recovery. I hadn't thought about it a lot—although, at the time, I was a smoker and had tried to quit a number of times and couldn't seem to. I was sort of baffled by that."

That one-off visit developed into an ongoing relationship with the group and sparked a long-term interest in the philosophy of addiction. It also played a vital role in Kent's journey back to the Christian faith of his revival-minister grandparents, something he'd abandoned during college, and fostered a concern to help the church support and learn from those battling addiction. "I had a pretty powerful experience in AA. I think it was partly because I had been away from the church for so long and become so cynical and hardened, that the vulnerability, the clear display of love, was gripping to me. So, I just started going to AA more regularly with McDermott. They knew that I wasn't an alcoholic, and I mostly just listened. It was part of how I eventually found my way back to the church and back to faith. It was a reminder of the church at its best."

Fifth and finally, if we want to create addiction-preventing, recovery-affirming church communities, we should rethink our approach to small groups. In the May 2019 edition of *Christianity*

Today, Kent considers a question many of us who have been part of recovery communities have asked: Would our small groups be more effective if they looked more like AA, mimicking its vulnerability, directness, and urgency?

It's not quite that simple, of course. "One unavoidable difference," Kent writes, "has to do with motivation. Most people go to AA because they are desperate. Much of the disarming candor and vulnerability characteristic of AA meetings is the fruit of desperation." Another key difference has to do with AA's anonymity. "Since AA groups are independent, members rarely encounter one another in other social circles. . . . Small groups, by contrast, normally know one another from church, and the natural (and good) human impulse toward displaying consistent character across different contexts makes radical candor far less likely."[6]

Would our small groups be more effective if they looked more like AA?

Those critical differences cannot be ignored. However, they suggest there is scope for "anonymous" church small groups for those who, for whatever reason, feel "desperate." Such a group could prove beneficial, not just to those battling addictions but also to members struggling with other issues that they don't want to disclose more widely (e.g., mental health issues or recovering from childhood sexual abuse). They also highlight the need, across church life, especially in small groups, for the presumption of confidentiality and a fierce commitment to maintaining it. Such groups would satisfy an acute need—not only felt by people in addiction—for the kind of vulnerable, genuine communication that produces life-giving relationships and sets people free.

Kent draws attention to several elements of AA meetings that, sensitively applied to church small groups, would foster the connection, community, and transformation we long to see. Three in particular warrant our attention.

First, we need to think about the set and setting. Does the form of our small groups align with their true purpose? Kent notes, "In linoleum-floored basement rooms, AA members sit on metal folding chairs around laminate tables with a pot of coffee, a stack of Styrofoam cups, and a box of store-bought cookies for refreshment. This drab simplicity is not an accident but rather an aesthetic complement to the meeting's purpose: welcoming the downtrodden; confessing failure, pain, and humiliation; and learning to find nourishment in hard places . . ."[7] In contrast, many church small groups have a social feel, a "food and fellowship" focus, that isn't conducive to vulnerability, honesty, and real depth of relationship.

Second, we need to prioritize *doing* over *thinking*. Kent writes, "At the heart of AA is the practice of the steps. The steps are simple to understand, though bracingly difficult to *do*. . . . AA is not a study group on addiction. It is a support group for spiritual practice."[8] How would church small groups look and feel if we shifted our focus from learning and talking about following Jesus to the nitty-gritty of doing life like Jesus? What would happen to our small groups if, in the place of a set of "steps," we agreed on a set of spiritual habits and focused our time on helping one another live them out day by day?

Third, we need to give fresh thought to leadership and participation. In the setting of a twelve-step group, leadership is light touch, and participation is voluntary. "Leadership rotates among the regulars and carries little onus because the meeting schedule is always the same," Kent observes. "Gather, open with a time of silence, read out the Serenity Prayer, invite everyone to introduce themselves, read 'How It Works' from the *Big Book*, read one of the Twelve Steps, open the floor for personal sharing, pass the donation basket around, pray the Lord's Prayer, gather around the refreshment table, go home. Night after night."[9]

This approach is why AA groups can meet so often. Almost anyone can lead the group. No special gifts are needed. No significant preparation is required. Instead, the focus of the gathering is its structure, the established content, and the participation of the members. Speaking is, however, entirely voluntary, and no one is pressured to contribute. The only expectation is that you introduce yourself and listen. "It would be a beautiful thing if small groups adopted this rule," Kent argues. "Often we are tired, we have nothing inside of us to share, yet we need the support of being close to others on the same path and hearing from those who feel inspired to share."[10]

UNWITTING PROPHET

As we discuss addiction and recovery in the sanctuary of his corner office at Biola, perhaps the most challenging insight I hear from Kent is the suggestion that in the life of the addict, we encounter an "unwitting prophet" who represents an unsettling challenge for the church.[11]

"Like the prophets of old, today's addicts may remind us our desire for God is trivial and weak, and our horizons of hope and expectancy are limited and mundane. We recoil at the presence of addicts, for we fear their life reveals the insufficiency of our own lives. . . . We recognize our own lives are not interesting and beautiful enough to offer a genuine alternative to the addict, and we fear a gospel powerful enough to redeem the addict would also threaten our own lives of decent and decorous mediocrity. We're not sure we want the church to be a place where persons with addictions are liberated since that would mean the church is no longer compatible with our own lives."[12] The prophet unsettles. His voice is always an interruption. His message is often unwelcome. But, in this case, the prophet speaks truth we need to hear.

As God's people in the age of addiction, we face two questions. The first relates to strategy and tactics. How do we become transformational communities of spiritual, emotional, relational, and physical flourishing—beacons of hope amid a worldwide addiction epidemic? The specifics of our responses to that question will depend on the particulars of our churches and their context. As we search for these specifics together, one thing must be uppermost in our minds: the pursuit of greater depth in our relationships with God and one another.

Is the church the age of addiction needs the kind of church to which I want to belong?

The second question is the harder of the two. It's a question of desire. Do I want to go deeper with God and deeper with His people? "Are we willing and ready to be a church that embodies this message and mission?"[13] Do I want my church to become a Rat Park church? Is the church the age of addiction needs the kind of church to which I want to belong? "The good news of the gospel," Kent challenges us, "is Jesus came not for those who are healthy but for those who are sick. He came to bring sight to the blind, release to the captive, liberation to the oppressed . . . and new life to the addict."[14]

Conclusion

TOGETHER IN THE WILDERNESS

WHITE LOBSTER

As Pedro, my Panga skipper, points behind him, I can't quite believe what I'm hearing. "Right there," he tells me, eyes alert and index finger pointing at a low spot on the beach, six feet behind us. "An old lady found twenty-five kilos of white lobster right here, just a few months ago." What did she do with it? "She sold it to one of the buyers." For how much? "They pay four to five thousand dollars a kilo."

Pedro and I are standing close to a rustic seafood restaurant on El Bluff Beach, a palm-lined strip of golden sand on Nicaragua's Mosquito Coast that stretches north, as far as the eye can see, towards the world's largest market for cocaine. El Bluff occupies a spit of land that shields Bluefields—once a safe haven for European buccaneers, now Nicaragua's largest Caribbean port—from the worst of the region's tropical storms. "White Lobster" is what Bluefields' population of Creoles, Miskitos, and Mestizos call the waterproof parcels of cocaine that, pitched overboard by "narcotraficantes" intercepted by navy patrol boats, wash up on these beaches.

"The drug trade is this city's blessing and its curse," writes NPR journalist Eyder Peralta.[1] "Eight out of ten people in this city are unemployed, yet there are stores everywhere, and business seems brisk." Captain Jose Echeverria, head of the port authority in Bluefields, concurs: "Somebody who fishes out a cocaine parcel would see it as a blessing from God, not a reason to alert the authorities. . . . but take poverty and joblessness, add easy money, and you get a bad mix."[2]

> **Could there be more that unites our stories than divides them?**

Many of the locals work for the traffickers as "lookouts, intelligence agents, and suppliers of gasoline for speedboats."[3] Payment for these services may be in cash or, as has become more common, in cocaine. "As a result," reports Bernd Debusmann for Reuters, "drug addiction has become a growing problem. . . . Crack is sold openly in several neighborhoods of Bluefields, where groups of young men waiting for customers stand in front of ramshackle houses. . . . There are at least 65 crack houses in the town" [population 55,000].[4]

As Pedro pilots us back across the bay's shallow brown waters, skillfully avoiding fishermen casting nets from wooden canoes and speedboats, heavy-laden with passengers on their way to the maritime communities that are dotted along the densely jungled coastline, I feel far away from the previous stops on my journey—from Huntington, Los Angeles, Canterbury, London, and even Santa Cruz, Bolivia.

So much distinguishes these places and peoples from one another. And yet, in the age of addiction, could there be more that unites their stories than divides them? They're connected by a global trade in illegal drugs that causes suffering at every step from production to consumption. Each place has unprecedented access to illegal and legal addictive experiences (e.g., alcohol, tobacco, gambling, gaming, and pornography) and correspondingly high levels of addictions of all kinds. They share in an experience of addiction and the suffering it inflicts on all whose lives it touches. The truth is, Bluefields is just one more frontline of the worldwide addiction epidemic—just another place where supply meets demand, addictions take root, and the vicious cycle of addiction visits suffering and heartbreak on individuals, families, and communities.

SIDE HUSTLE?

The day after my visit to El Bluff Beach, I spoke with Pastor Ed Jaentschke, who leads Verbo Church, a thriving community that meets in a large building perched on a hilltop with views across the city and bay below. Just home after a long drive back from a denominational gathering on the outskirts of Managua, Nicaragua's capital, Pastor Ed pours us a coffee and shares his rich experience of life in Bluefields.

Ed knows these parts well. He grew up further up the Caribbean coast in Puerto Cabezas and has pastored in Bluefields for decades. As we talk, it becomes clear that despite the city facing a serious addiction issue, there are few specialist services to help those in addiction, either locally or at a national level. Those that do exist, don't inspire much confidence. Under his leadership, the church has established outreach ministries that include a school, a feeding program for children, and a children's home. What can they do to help the alcoholics and drug addicts in the community find lasting freedom?

Your church may be located within a well-resourced and effective treatment system, or you may have little access to specialist addiction services. Either way, as the waves of the addiction epidemic crash onto our shores, we all face the same question. As churches, how do we respond to the challenges and opportunities presented by the age of addiction? For the sake of those among us who are at risk of addiction, in active addiction itself, and in recovery from addiction—there are six things we can do.

First, we must engage with the addiction issue. A signature feature of the modern world should not remain relegated to the margins of the church's collective consciousness. Nor should it be outsourced entirely to specialist services, even those who operate with a Christian ethos, or considered a purely "medical" issue beyond the church's purview. Addiction needs to be one of the church's core concerns, not a side hustle.

Second, we need to understand addiction and recovery better. Church leaders, particularly those leading small groups, preaching, teaching, and working with young people, need to be addiction-aware and recovery-sensitive. As part of this, we'll benefit immensely from turning for help to those in our communities with experience of addiction. The more we hear from those with personal experience of addictions of all types and all degrees of severity, along with family members and specialists, the better.

Third, we need to establish healthy partnerships with addiction specialists and services in the wider community. This will include statutory services and those provided by the private and charitable sectors. As an active member of the addiction care network, we can effectively engage with the needs we encounter both in our churches and the wider community. As we do this, we should be quick to see opportunities to use our resources generously, for example, by offering a comfortable meeting place to mutual-aid groups like AA or encouraging our members to support the work of Christian charities working in the addiction field.

Fourth, we need to explore how we can directly contribute to the recovery capital available to those in and outside of our churches. What role could my church play in the fight against addiction? Does the wider community lack information about addiction services?

Perhaps we could create a website to help people find the help and support they need. Can our members afford the therapy they need to address their addiction? Perhaps we could establish a free-of-charge counseling service or create a fund to help pay for therapy. Do those leaving treatment programs have training and employment opportunities? Perhaps we could encourage the business owners in the local Christian community to get involved.

Fifth, we need to sensitively reach out to those looking for life-giving solutions to the problems produced by a world of despair, desolation, adversity, and disconnection. As God's people, we are called to help slaves to addiction become children of the living God and family in the community of God. In the "Spider-Man" stuff of the gospel and in a recovery-sensitive church community that supports those engaging with the "Batman" stuff of recovery, we hold in our hands an escape ladder out of addiction and into abundant life.

> **We are called to help slaves to addiction become children of the living God and family in the community of God.**

Sixth and finally, we need to go deeper with God and with one another. Churches characterized by anemic spirituality and superficial relationships provide little of genuine value to those fighting off the siren call of a bottle, syringe, or hook-up app. This isn't a matter of style, as if spiritual and relational depth is only possible if you sing the right songs or pray in the right way. It's a matter of substance and a challenge to us all.

NO SHORTCUT

Born in Toyko in 1929, at the dawn of the Great Depression, theologian Kosuke Koyama's academic career would take him from New Jersey to Thailand, Singapore, New Zealand, and finally back to the

US. In 1979, more than a decade before the internet became publicly available, Koyama wrote a book called *Three Mile An Hour God*, in which he contrasts the instant efficiency of modern technology with God's way of teaching people—a style characterized by the forty years his people spent walking in the wilderness where the learning was slow, difficult, and rooted in their daily experience.

"God walks 'slowly' because he is love," Koyama writes. "If he is not love, he would have gone much faster. Love has its speed. It is an inner speed. It is a different kind of speed from the technological speed to which we are accustomed. It is slow. . . . It goes on in the depth of our life, whether we notice or not, whether we are currently hit by storm or not, at three miles an hour. It is the speed we walk and therefore it is the speed the love of God walks."[5]

"God walks 'slowly' because He is love."

The whole exodus narrative, describing as it does a slavery born of the need for the provision of basic unmet needs (grain in a time of famine), a painful liberation, and a long journey through the wilderness to the promised land, provides a rich biblical context for thinking about recovery from sin in all forms, including addiction. It speaks to us of a God whose way of working often feels painfully slow—a pace that makes no sense in our world of instant-everything—but who walks with us, meeting our needs one day at a time, as we journey through the wilderness. In the people's longing to return to the fettered security of life in Egypt, we see the yearning to relapse into a hibernated state. In the promise of a land flowing with milk and honey, distant but getting closer, we see the dreams of those who long to be fully satisfied by God's presence and provision alone.

As we walk beside those who are on this journey in the wilderness, there is, as we have seen, much we can do to help them find ever-greater confidence to live clean and sober. A community, not lone rangers, is the best source of this support. The demands are too great, and the needs too diverse, for one person to deliver them alone. But, behind all the doing, whom should we be? What qualities must we develop if we are to help in a way that's both effective and sustainable?

Above all, we must be patient and commit to the long haul. We must accept the fact that God walks slowly, even if we don't understand or like it. In all but the most exceptional of circumstances, recovery is a slow, faltering process of change. Those who accompany others on this journey need to adjust their expectations and approach accordingly. "There is no shortcut to the promised land," writes Timothy McMahan King. "If someone tells you there is one, you can know the land they are offering is a mirage. This is not to say that there isn't a goal or a destination. There is. The journey is not the destination. But the journey is the place that transforms the wanderer so that the destination might truly be seen. . . . Our impatience can destroy us. Our demand for results now can poison us. The fastest is not always the best. The most expedient is not the greatest."[6]

In addition to patience, we will need compassion. In *The Heart of Recovery*, Deborah and David Beddoe share the story of their fifteen-year battle with Dave's prescription drug addiction, highlighting the instrumental role played by their compassionate church family.

"The community that caught my family and me when I fell wasn't made up of a perfect pastor, family, or church that had it all figured out," writes Dave. "Our safety net was held by people who were willing to respond with compassion and reexamine what they thought they knew about addiction and addicts and this idea of 'recovery.' Family and friends who wrestled intensely with forgiveness and continued to try to love an addict, even when he broke their hearts. A wife who was willing to practice the countercultural idea of forgiving seventy times seven. And a broader community of broken people who welcomed me as a brother. . . . Hope began in community through the compassion of a group of bystanders who were willing to move past the stink of our lives and do what they could to help."[7]

CAREGIVING

Next, whether you're a church leader, a worker in the addiction care field, a family member, or a friend, you will need clarity to perceive the limits of your capacity and responsibility. The charity I lead, Novō Communities, exists to bring new life to individuals, peace to families, and hope to communities gripped by addiction. How do we do that? By empowering God's people in developing nations to create transformational communities that offer healing, wholeness, and hope. This statement of vision and mission helps lift our eyes beyond all the demands of the moment. It reminds us why we do what we do and challenges us to action. It is also a vital reminder that there is a vast gap between what we desire—new life, peace, and hope for those gripped by addiction—and what we can make happen. We can't transform lives. We can't set captives free. We can't restore families. What we can do is *offer* healing, wholeness, and hope to those who join our residential communities. The rest is in the hands of God and the individual.

In this context, the distinction that philosopher Martin Heidegger draws between two distinct ways of caring for others, "caretaking" and "caregiving," is helpful. When we are caretaking, we do things for others so that they don't have to do them for themselves. Caretaking is about protecting, providing, and solving on behalf of others. In contrast, caregiving "does not take the cares off the shoulders of its recipients. Instead, caregiving gives its recipients their own cares. It literally helps care receivers to pick up their own burdens and hoist them on their own shoulders. By leaping ahead and clearing the way, caregiving makes it possible for the care receiver to assume his or her own proper, personal care. Enabling disables. . . . In contrast, caregiving makes possible. It empowers."[8]

Finally, as we walk alongside those in recovery, in addition to patience, compassion, and clarity, we will need unwavering hope. Addiction care calls for steadfast confidence in the God who specializes in working in the wilderness, a resource we can't muster for ourselves. Instead, it comes as a gift as we spend time in God's presence.

"As a culture and as a church," observe Deborah and David Beddoe, "we've taken *we can't change people* to mean *people don't change.* And we've taken *we can't change people* to mean *there's nothing we can do to help them change.*" The problems with this are threefold. "When we buy the idea that people don't change," they explain, "we deny both the human capacity for change and the power of God to change the human heart. And maybe, most tragic of all, we free ourselves of the discomfort of close relationship with someone who needs us, effectively abandoning the mission God has set right in front of us. Grace allows time and space for transformation. People do change. People consumed by addiction can recover. . . . But it's a process. We forget this. It doesn't happen overnight. Recovery takes endurance."[9]

LEAD US HOME

There is hope in addiction. Hope for freedom, restoration, a fresh start, and a different ending. Hope for now and hope for eternity. Recovery *is* possible.

On the streets of Skid Row, where our journey began, Row Church's service concluded with the singing of *Amazing Grace*, a favorite hymn of that community and so many in addiction and recovery. Together, we stood and sang of Jesus, and His grace, a grace that will "lead us home." Here and now, there is so much that we can do to help addicted people find healing, wholeness, and hope. However, ultimate hope in addiction looks beyond today's horizons in the wilderness to the return of Christ, the consummation of His kingdom, and the first sunrise in the promised land:

> I saw the Holy City, the new Jerusalem, coming down out of heaven from God, prepared as a bride beautifully dressed for her husband. And I heard a loud voice from the throne saying, "Look! God's dwelling place is now among the people, and he will dwell with them. They will be his people, and God himself will be with them and be their God. He will wipe every tear from their eyes. There will be no more death or mourning or crying or pain, for the old order of things has passed away." (Rev. 21:2–4)

Acknowledgments

I owe a tremendous debt of gratitude to a wonderful group of people whose collective insight, experience, encouragement, and prayers have brought this book to life.

First and foremost, I want to thank those who have allowed me to share their stories and the stories of their communities: Tom Keller, Huseyin Djemil, Andy and Rachel Day, Jana Stoner, Mayor Steve Williams, Pastor Cue Jn-Marie, Professor Kent Dunnington, Pastor Ed Jaentschke, Benigno Huarachi, Jorge DeLemos, Tim Wheatley, Keith McAree, Rick Mills, Neil Warburton, and Mark and Jenny Burrows. I'm profoundly grateful to each of you for giving this book its heart.

Misty Lopez, Lewis Longard, Simon Benham, Chris Short, Derek Tidball, Kevin Lancaster, and Jon Dale each invested substantial time reading and commenting on draft chapters, adding tremendously to the quality of the final manuscript, and encouraging me along the way. I owe you! I'm also indebted to the brilliant men and women who blessed this book with their endorsement, and to John Burke and Brian Brunson for a foreword rooted in the pastor's heart and the grace of God.

In commissioning the book, Dr. Bryan Litfin believed in this project, and its author, before there was much evidence to justify his confidence. I'm thankful to him for doing so and to Duane Sherman, Phil Newman, John Hinkley, and the team at Moody Publishers for the quality and warmth of their editorial support.

More broadly, three groups of people deserve my heartfelt thanks. First, the staff and residents of Novō Communities and

Yeldall Manor. Second, Trevor Childs and Novō's UK trustees. Third, Sharon Klitgaard and the incredible group that gathers monthly on Zoom to support our family and Novō's ministry in prayer. Together, their impact on my life and this book is beyond calculation.

I want to honor my incredible family. In 1982, my parents, Dave and Sue Partington, responded to God's calling and moved their family on-site at Yeldall Manor, then a fledging residential rehab founded by Bill and Joanie Yoder. Over many years, God has used them to express the the reality of grace and the Father's heart both to those in recovery and those with a calling to help them find freedom.

My wife, Mickey, has been a constant source of love and grace throughout the writing process and the best of companions on a journey that has required more faith and courage than we would ever have imagined when we began our life together. She also gave the book a title that perfectly captures its message! Our kids—Daniel, Jemimah, Phoebe, JJ, and Miah—are an absolute joy, and it is to them that I dedicate this book.

Bibliography

Alexander, Bruce. *The Globalization of Addiction: A Study in Poverty of the Spirit* (Oxford: Oxford University Press, 2008).

Alter, Adam. *Irresistible: Why We Can't Stop Checking, Scrolling, Clicking and Watching* (London: Vintage, 2017).

Beddoe, Deborah and David. *The Heart of Recovery: How Compassion and Community Offer Hope in the Wake of Addiction* (Grand Rapids: Revell, 2019).

Benz, Jonathan. *The Recovery-Minded Church: Loving and Ministering to People with Addiction* (Downers Grove: IVP, 2016).

Brand, Russell. *Recovery: Freedom from Our Addictions* (London: Bluebird, 2017).

Burroughs, William. *Junky: The Definitive Text of "Junk"* (London: Penguin, 2003).

Case, Anne and Deaton, Angus. *Deaths of Despair and the Future of Capitalism* (Princeton: Princeton University Press, 2020).

Comer, John Mark. *The Ruthless Elimination of Hurry* (Colorado Springs: Waterbrook, 2019).

Courtwright, David. *The Age of Addiction: How Bad Habits Became Big Business* (Cambridge: Harvard University Press, 2019).

Duhigg, Charles. *The Power of Habit: Why We Do What We Do in Life and Business* (New York: Random House, 2012).

Dunnington, Kent. *Addiction and Virtue: Beyond the Models of Disease and Choice* (Downers Grove: IVP, 2011).

Eyal, Nir. *Indistractable: How to Control Your Attention and Choose Your Life* (Dallas: BenBella Books, 2019).

Foulkes, Lucy. *Losing Our Minds: The Challenge of Defining Mental Illness* (New York: St. Martin's Press, 2021).

Grisel, Judith. *Never Enough: The Neuroscience and Experience of Addiction* (New York: Anchor Books, 2019).

Haines, Seth. *Coming Clean: A Story of Faith* (Grand Rapids: Zondervan, 2015).

Hari, Johann. *Chasing the Scream: The First and Last Days of the War on Drugs* (London: Bloomsbury, 2015).

Hart, Carl. *High Price: Drugs, Neuroscience and Discovering Myself* (New York: Harper Perennial, 2014).

King, Timothy McMahan. *Addiction Nation: What the Opioid Crisis Reveals About Us* (Harrisonburg: Herald Press, 2019).

Knapp, Caroline. *Drinking: A Love Story* (New York: Bantam Dell, 1996).

Lewis, Marc. *Memoirs of an Addicted Brain: A Neuroscientist Examines His Former Life on Drugs* (New York: PublicAffairs, 2011).

Lewis, Marc. *The Biology of Desire* (New York: PublicAffairs, 2015).

Marlowe, Ann. *How to Stop Time: Heroin from A to Z* (New York: Basic Books, 1999).

Maté, Gabor. *In the Realm of Hungry Ghosts: Close Encounters with Addiction* (Berkeley: North Atlantic Books, 2008).

May, Gerald. *Addiction and Grace: Love and Spirituality in the Healing of Addictions* (New York: HarperCollins, 1988).

McIntosh, James and McKeganey, Neil. *Beating the Dragon: The Recovery from Dependent Drug Use* (London: Routledge, 2002).

Orford, Jim. *Excessive Appetites: A Psychological View of Addictions* (Chichester: John Wiley & Sons, 2001).

Peele, Stanton. *The Addiction Experience* (Center City: Hazelden, 1977).

Peele, Stanton and Brodsky, Archie. *Love and Addiction* (New York: Taplinger Publishing, 1975).

Quinones, Sam. *Dreamland: The True Tale of America's Opiate Epidemic* (New York: Bloomsbury, 2015).

Vance, J. D. *Hillbilly Elegy: A Memoir of a Family and Culture in Crisis* (New York: HarperCollins, 2016).

West, Robert and Brown, Jamie. *Theory of Addiction* (Chichester: Wiley Blackwell, 2013).

White, Aaron. *Recovering: From Brokenness and Addiction to Blessedness and Community* (Grand Rapids: Baker Academic, 2020).

Willard, Dallas. *The Spirit of the Disciplines: Understanding How God Changes Lives* (New York: HarperCollins, 1999).

Notes

Introduction: On the Shadow Side

1. Tuen Voeten, "Skid Row: Inside the Epicentre of LA's Homeless and Crystal Meth Crisis," *Independent*, October 10, 2021, independent.co.uk/arts-entertainment/photography/skid-row-la-homeless-crystal-meth-crisis-b1934786.html.
2. The Council of Economic Advisers, "The State of Homelessness in America," September 2019, nhipdata.org/local/upload/file/The-State-of-Homelessness-in-America.pdf.
3. Howard Stutz, "Gaming Revenues of $13.4 Billion Statewide, $7 Billion on the Strip Set Records," Nevada Independent, January 27, 2022, https://thenevadaindependent.com/article/gaming-revenues-of-13-4-billion-statewide-7-billion-on-the-strip-set-records.
4. Estimate provided by Craig Hettinger, CEO of the Huntington Addiction Wellness Center, in an interview with the author, February 5, 2020.
5. Russell Brand, *Recovery: Freedom from Our Addictions* (London: Bluebird Books for Life, 2018), 220. Kindle.

Chapter 1: One in Five

1. Aircraft Accident Report, National Transportation Safety Board, April 14, 1972, https://www.ntsb.gov/investigations/AccidentReports/Reports/AAR7211.pdf.
2. Interview with the author, February 4, 2020.
3. Division of Addiction Sciences in the Department of Family and Community Health at the Marshall University Joan C. Edwards School of Medicine, "The City of Solutions: A Guidebook to What Works (and What Does Not) in Reducing the Impact of Substance Use on Local Communities," May 2021, 7. jcesom.marshall.edu/media/60482/coh-guidebook-2021.pdf.
4. Suspected overdose and naloxone use data provided by Connie Priddy, Director of Quality Compliance/Huntington QRT Program Coordinator, Cabell County EMS, via email, May 14, 2020.
5. Timothy McMahan King, *Addiction Nation: What the Opioid Crisis Reveals About Us* (Harrisonburg: Herald Press, 2019), loc. 215. Kindle.
6. cdc.gov/nchs/pressroom/nchs_press_releases/2021/20211117.htm.
7. cdc.gov/opioids/basics/fentanyl.html.
8. nytimes.com/interactive/2017/06/05/upshot/opioid-epidemic-drug-overdose-deaths-are-rising-faster-than-ever.html.
9. edition.cnn.com/2021/11/17/health/drug-overdose-deaths-record-high/index.html.

10. statnews.com/2017/06/27/opioid-deaths-forecast/.
11. pbs.org/newshour/nation/many-americans-died-u-s-wars.
12. Timothy McMahan King, *Addiction Nation: What the Opioid Crisis Reveals About Us* (Harrisonburg: Herald Press, 2019), loc. 206. Kindle.
13. Substance Abuse and Mental Health Services Administration (SAMHSA), "Key Substance Use and Mental Health Indicators in the United States: Results from the 2020 National Survey on Drug Use and Health," 4, samhsa.gov/data/sites/default/files/reports/rpt35325/NSDUHFFRPDFWHTMLFiles2020/2020NSDUHFFR1PDFW102121.pdf.
14. Hannah Ritchie and Max Roser, "Alcohol Consumption," April 2018, revised January 2022, ourworldindata.org/alcohol-consumption.
15. Hannah Ritchie and Max Roser, "Opioids, Cocaine, Cannabis and Illicit Drugs," 2022, ourworldindata.org/illicit-drug-use.
16. Hannah Ritchie and Max Roser, "Drug Use," 2019, ourworldindata.org/drug-use.
17. Jakob Mathey et al., "Global Alcohol Exposure Between 1990 and 2017 and Forecasts Until 2030: A Modelling Study," *The Lancet* 393, no. 10190 (June 22, 2019): thelancet.com/journals/lancet/article/PIIS0140-6736(18)32744-2/fulltext.
18. National Institutes of Health, "Trends in U.S. Methamphetamine Use and Associated Deaths," October 5, 2021, www.nih.gov/news-events/nih-research-matters/trends-us-methamphetamine-use-associated-deaths.
19. United Nations, "Executive Summary," *World Drug Report 2019*, wdr.unodc.org/wdr2019/en/exsum.html.
20. Rob Ralphs et al., "Adding Spice to the Porridge: The Development of a Synthetic Cannabinoid Market in an English Prison," *International Journal of Drug Policy* 40 (February 2017): 57–69, sciencedirect.com/science/article/pii/S0955395916303073#bib0060.
21. Mike Power, "Spice Is More Than a Deadly Drug—It's a Window on Our Society," *The Guardian*, October 29, 2019, theguardian.com/cities/2019/oct/29/spice-so-called-zombie-drug-uk-poorest-communities.
22. Laura Salm-Reifferscheidt, "Tramadol: The Opioid Taking Over Africa," *Independent*, August 12, 2019. independent.co.uk/news/long_reads/health-and-wellbeing/tramadol-opioid-africa-drugs-togo-a9010916.html.
23. Hannah Ritchie and Max Roser, "Smoking," first published in May 2013, partly updated January 2022, ourworldindata.org/smoking.
24. Steve Sussman et al, "Prevalence of the Addictions: A Problem of the Majority or the Minority?," *Evaluation and the Health Professions* 34, no. 1 (September 27, 2010): 3–5, ncbi.nlm.nih.gov/pmc/articles/PMC3134413/.
25. Marc Lewis, *The Biology of Desire: Why Addiction Is Not a Disease* (New York: PublicAffairs, 2015), loc. 427, 2408. Kindle.
26. Judith Grisel, *Never Enough: The Neuroscience and Experience of Addiction* (New York: Anchor Books, 2019), 3. Kindle.
27. James McIntosh and Neil McKeganey, *Beating the Dragon: The Recovery from Dependent Drug Use* (London: Routledge, 2002), 35.
28. Ibid., 36.

29. Ibid., 48–49.
30. Ibid., 49.
31. Ibid., 39.
32. Ibid., 65.
33. Ibid., 65–66.
34. Gallup, "Alcohol and Drinking," news.gallup.com/poll/1582/alcohol-drinking.aspx.
35. Child Welfare Information Gateway, "Parental Substance Use: A Primer for Child Welfare Professionals," January 2021, 3. childwelfare.gov/pubs/factsheets/parentalsubuse/.
36. National Center on Substance Abuse and Child Welfare, "Child Welfare and Alcohol and Drug Use Statistics," ncsacw.samhsa.gov/research/child-welfare-and-treatment-statistics.aspx.
37. Substance Abuse and Mental Health Services Administration (SAMHSA), "2018 National Survey on Drug Use and Health: Women," 30. samhsa.gov/data/sites/default/files/reports/rpt23250/5_Women_2020_01_14_508.pdf.
38. Child Welfare Information Gateway, "Parental Substance Use: A Primer for Child Welfare Professionals," January 2021, 3. childwelfare.gov/pubs/factsheets/parentalsubuse/.
39. McIntosh and McKeganey, *Beating the Dragon*, 79.
40. Ibid., 78.
41. Ibid., 79.
42. Stanton Peele, "Addiction in Society" blog header. psychologytoday.com/ie/blog/addiction-in-society.
43. Lifeway research, "Half of Pastors See Opioid Abuse in Their Own Congregations," November 19, 2019. lifewayresearch.com/2019/11/19/half-of-pastors-see-opioid-abuse-in-their-own-congregations/.
44. Barna Group, "The Porn Phenomenon," February 5, 2016. barna.com/the-porn-phenomenon/#.VqZoN_krIdU.
45. Barna group research for Proven Men. provenmen.org/wp-content/uploads/2016/09/Survey-eBook-no-links-Linked.pdf?utm_source=Newsletter&utm_medium=email&utm_content=Thanks+for+downloading&utm_campaign=Porn+Survey&vgo_ee=D9ZiVGl%2Bk0RoDbZhOYhio3mtjWGMMj0BWmcmPWC3iqU%3D.

Chapter 2: When Supply Meets Demand

1. Katherine Pyles, "Remembering Adam Johnson," *Huntington Quarterly*, September 28, 2018. huntingtonquarterly.com/2018/09/28/issue-94-remembering-adam-johnson/.
2. Curtis Johnson, "The Victims," *The Herald-Dispatch*, November 17, 2017. herald-dispatch.com/news/the-victims/article_7c565cae-8a98-53f6-b12b-73226544da45.html.
3. Pyles, "Remembering . . ."
4. Congressional Research Service, "Heroin Trafficking in the United States," February 14, 2019, 2. fas.org/sgp/crs/misc/R44599.pdf.

5. Sam Quinones, *Dreamland: The True Tale of America's Opiate Epidemic* (New York: Bloomsbury, 2015), 43–44. Kindle.
6. "Johnson & Johnson, one of the best-known American pharmaceutical companies, supplied most of the raw material for opioid painkillers in the US from a subsidiary, Tasmanian Alkaloids, which grew poppies on farms in Tasmania . . . At a time when the American military was bombing the opium supply in Helmand province in Afghanistan, Johnson & Johnson was legally growing the raw material for the nation's opioid supply in Tasmania." Anne Case and Angus Deaton, *Deaths of Despair and the Future of Capitalism* (Princeton: Princeton University Press, 2020), 125. Kindle.
7. Minnesota Department of Health, "Perception of Pain." health.state.mn.us/communities/opioids/prevention/painperception.html.
8. norc.org/NewsEventsPublications/PressReleases/Pages/one-third-of-americans-have-received-an-opioid-prescription-in-the-past-two-years.aspx
9. Centers for Disease Control (CDC), "Prescription Opioid Death Maps," cdc.gov/drugoverdose/deaths/prescription/maps.html.
10. Anne Case and Angus Deaton, *Deaths of Despair and the Future of Capitalism* (Princeton: Princeton University Press, 2020), 124. Kindle.
11. Ibid., 113, 119.
12. Sean Illing, "Capitalism Is Turning Us into Addicts," Vox, April 18, 2020, vox.com/science-and-health/2019/10/17/18647521/capitalism-age-of-addiction-phone-david-courtwright.
13. David Courtwright, *The Age of Addiction: How Bad Habits Became Big Business* (Cambridge: Harvard University Press, 2019), loc.185. Kindle.
14. Julia Belluz, "Juul, the Vape Device Teens Are Getting Hooked On, Explained," Vox, December 20, 2018, vox.com/science-and-health/2018/5/1/17286638/juul-vaping-e-cigarette.
15. Sarah Boseley et al, "How Children Around the World are Exposed to Cigarette Advertising," *The Guardian*, March 9, 2018. theguardian.com/world/2018/mar/09/how-children-around-the-world-are-exposed-to-cigarette-advertising.
16. National Council on Problem Gambling, "A Review of Sports Wagering & Gambling Addiction Studies: Executive Summary," ncpgambling.org/wp-content/uploads/2020/01/Sports-gambling_NCPGLitRvwExecSummary.pdf.
17. Adam Alter, *Irresistible: Why We Can't Stop Checking, Scrolling, Clicking and Watching* (London: Vintage, 2017), 78. Kindle.
18. Ibid., 3.
19. Alvin M. Shuster, "G.I. Heroin Addiction Epidemic in Vietnam," *The New York Times*, May 16, 1971. nytimes.com/1971/05/16/archives/gi-heroin-addiction-epidemic-in-vietnam-gi-heroin-addiction-is.html.
20. Anne Case and Angus Deaton, *Deaths of Despair and the Future of Capitalism* (Princeton: Princeton University Press, 2020), 122. Kindle.
21. Johann Hari, *Chasing the Scream: The First and Last Days of the War on Drugs* (London: Bloomsbury, 2015), loc. 3397. Kindle.
22. *Irresistible*, 48.
23. Case and Deaton, *Deaths of Despair*, 122.

24. Lee N. Robins et al., "Narcotic Use in Southeast Asia and Afterward: An Interview Study of 898 Vietnam Returnees," *Archives of General Psychiatry* 32, no. 8 (1975): 955–61.
25. Case and Deaton, *Deaths of Despair*, 122.
26. Courtwright, *The Age of Addiction*, loc. 191.
27. *Encyclopaedia Brittannica Online*, s.v. "anomie," britannica.com/topic/anomie, May 27, 2020, britannica.com/topic/anomie.
28. Hari, *Chasing the Scream*, 3397.
29. Alter, *Irresistible*, 47.
30. Lee Robins, "Vietnam Veterans' Rapid Recovery From Heroin Addiction: A Fluke or a Normal Expectation?," *Addiction*, 88, 1049.
31. Dan Baum, *Smoke and Mirrors: The War on Drugs and the Politics of Failure* (Boston: Little, Brown & Company, 1996) 62.
32. Division of Addiction Sciences in the Department of Family and Community Health at the Marshall University Joan C. Edwards School of Medicine, "The City of Solutions: A Guidebook to What Works (and What Does Not) in Reducing the Impact of Substance Use on Local Communities," May 2021, 4, jcesom.marshall.edu/media/60482/coh-guide-book-2021.pdf.
33. Marshall Health, "The Road to Recovery," https://www.marshallhealth.org/services/addiction-medicine/the-road-to-recovery/.
34. "Huntington Mayor Tells Drug Dealers to Get Out," *West Virginia Press*, August 6, 2014, wvpress.org/copydesk/insight/huntington-mayor-tells-drug-dealers-get/.
35. Division of Addiction Sciences in the Department of Family and Community Health at the Marshall University Joan C. Edwards School of Medicine, "The City of Solutions: A Guidebook to What Works (and What Does Not) in Reducing the Impact of Substance Use on Local Communities," May 2021, 6, jcesom.marshall.edu/media/60482/coh-guide-book-2021.pdf.
36. Melanie Shafer, "Looking at the Cabell County Quick Response Team's Impact on Overdose Deaths," *WSAZ News*, December 8, 2021, wsaz.com/2021/12/08/looking-cabell-county-quick-response-teams-impact-overdose-deaths/.
37. Avram Goldstein, "Heroin Maintenance: A Medical View," *Journal of Drug Issues*, 9, 342. Referenced by Bruce Alexander, *The Globalization of Addiction: A Study in Poverty of the Spirit* (Oxford: Oxford University Press, 2008), 193–94.
38. Bruce Alexander, *The Globalization of Addiction: A Study in Poverty of the Spirit* (Oxford: Oxford University Press, 2008), 194.
39. An image of a Skinner box and Rat Park can be found at brucekalexander.com/articles-speeches/rat-park/148-addiction-the-view-from-rat-park.
40. Alexander, *The Globalization of Addition*, 195.
41. Ibid.
42. Jim Orford, Emeritus Professor of Clinical and Community Psychology at the University of Birmingham, uses this language to describe addictions. Jim

Orford, *Excessive Appetites: A Psychological View of Addictions* (Chichester: John Wiley & Sons, 2001).
43. Hari, *Chasing the Scream*, 3385.
44. Alexander, *The Globalization of Addiction*, 163.

Chapter 3: Despair & Emptiness

1. Ann Marlowe, *How to Stop Time: Heroin from A to Z* (New York: Basic Books, 1999), loc. 501. Kindle.
2. Sam Quinones, *Dreamland: The True Tale of America's Opiate Epidemic* (New York: Bloomsbury, 2015), 18–19.
3. "Deaths of Despair and the Future of Capitalism," Princeton University Press, press.princeton.edu/books/hardcover/9780691190785/deaths-of-despair-and-the-future-of-capitalism..
4. Anne Case and Angus Deaton, *Deaths of Despair and the Future of Capitalism* (Princeton: Princeton University Press, 2020), 94. They further explain: "Deaths of despair among white men and women aged forty-five to fifty-four rose from thirty per one hundred thousand in 1990 to ninety-two per one hundred thousand in 2017. In every US state, suicide mortality rates for whites aged forty-five to fifty-four increased between 1999–2000 and 2016–17. In all but two states, mortality rates from alcoholic liver disease rose. And in every state, drug overdose mortality rates increased" (40).
5. "Deaths of Despair and the Future of Capitalism," Princeton University Press, press.princeton.edu/books/hardcover/9780691190785/deaths-of-despair-and-the-future-of-capitalism.
6. J. D. Vance, *Hillbilly Elegy: A Memoir of a Family and Culture in Crisis* (New York: HarperCollins, 2016), 1–2.
7. Johann Hari, *Chasing the Scream: The First and Last Days of the War on Drugs* (London: Bloomsbury, 2015), loc. 4499. Kindle.
8. Pascal, *Pensées VII*, 425 (Gianluca, 2017), loc. 1645. Kindle.
9. *Yeldall Manor Newsletter*, Autumn 2018.
10. *Yeldall Manor Newsletter*, Summer 2019.
11. Ann Marlowe, *How to Stop Time: Heroin from A to Z* (New York: Basic Books, 1999), 155.
12. Bruce Alexander, quoted by Johann Hari, *Chasing the Scream: The First and Last Days of the War on Drugs* (London: Bloomsbury, 2015), loc. 3456. Kindle.
13. This point was well illustrated in the summer of 2020. After the end of the UK's COVID-19 lockdown, the Chancellor of Exchequer, Rishi Sunak, eager to stimulate public spending, implored the British people to "eat out to help out." bbc.com/news/business-53911505.
14. Hari, *Chasing the Scream,* loc. 3558.
15. Timothy McMahan King, *Addiction Nation: What the Opioid Crisis Reveals About Us* (Harrisonburg: Herald Press, 2019), loc. 194. Kindle.
16. Jimmy Carter, "Energy and National Goals: Address to the Nation," July 15, 1979, jimmycarterlibrary.gov/assets/documents/speeches/energy-crisis.phtml.
17. Ibid.

Chapter 4: Adversity & Disconnection

1. Gobierno Autónomo Departamental Santa Cruz, "Censo de Personas en Situactió de Calle 2018," Santa Cruz de la Sierra, Bolivia, 1.
2. Ibid., 3–4.
3. Stanton Peele, *The Addiction Experience* (Center City: Hazelden, 1977), loc. 85. Kindle.
4. Vincent J. Felitti, "The Origins of Addiction: Evidence from the Adverse Childhood Experiences Study," 2003, nijc.org/pdfs/Subject%20 Matter%20Articles/Drugs%20and%20Alc/ACE%20Study%20-%20 OriginsofAddiction.pdf.
5. Centers for Disease Control, "ACEs Definitions," *About the CDC-Kaiser ACE Study.* cdc.gov/violenceprevention/aces/about.html.
6. Centers for Disease Control, "ACEs Prevalence," *About the CDC-Kaiser ACE Study.* cdc.gov/violenceprevention/aces/about.html.
7. Vincent J. Felitti, "The Origins of Addiction: Evidence from the Adverse Childhood Experiences Study," 2003, 5–6, nijc.org/pdfs/Subject%20 Matter%20Articles/Drugs%20and%20Alc/ACE%20Study%20-%20 OriginsofAddiction.pdf.
8. Ibid., 3, 8.
9. *Yeldall Manor Newsletter,* Summer 2012.
10. *Yeldall Manor Newsletter,* Spring 2016.
11. The film *Step Inside the Circle* is available at compassionprisonproject.org.
12. Gabor Maté, *In the Realm of Hungry Ghosts: Close Encounters with Addiction* (Berkeley: North Atlantic Books, 2008), loc. 3664. Kindle.
13. Ibid., loc. 622.
14. Ibid., loc. 600.
15. unfairtobacco.org/en/corporations/china-national-tobacco-corporation/.
16. Koen van Gelder, "Global cigarette market share as of 2019, by company", January 13, 2022. statista.com/statistics/279873/global-cigarette-market-share-by-group/; Sarah Boseley et al., "How Children Around the World are Exposed to Cigarette Advertising," *The Guardian,* March 9, 2018 theguardian.com/world/2018/mar/09/how-children-around-the-world-are-exposed-to-cigarette-advertising.
17. Hannah Ritchie and Max Roser, "Smoking," January 2022. ourworldindata.org/smoking#smoking-is-one-of-the-leading-risks-for-early-death.
18. Joshua Wolf Shenk, "What Makes Us Happy?", *The Atlantic,* June 2009, theatlantic.com/magazine/archive/2009/06/what-makes-us-happy/307439/.
19. Ibid.
20. Ibid.
21. Liz Mineo, "Good genes are nice, but joy is better," *The Harvard Gazette,* April 11, 2017. news.harvard.edu/gazette/story/2017/04/over-nearly-80-years-harvard-study-has-been-showing-how-to-live-a-healthy-and-happy-life/.
22. Shenk, "What Makes Us Happy?"
23. Joshua Wolf Shenk confirms that John F. Kennedy was among that original cohort, though his files have been removed from the study's archives and have been sealed until 2040. Joshua Wolf Shenk, "What Makes Us Happy?,"

The Atlantic, June 2009, theatlantic.com/magazine/archive/2009/06/
what-makes-us-happy/307439/.
24. Michael Miller, "What Makes a Good Life?" 6seconds.org/2018/09/18/
what-makes-a-good-life-3-lessons-on-life-love-and-decision-making-from-
the-harvard-grant-study/.
25. Ibid.
26. John Donne, Meditation XVII, *The Works of John Donne*, Vol. III, (London:
John W. Parker, 1839), 574–575. luminarium.org/sevenlit/donne/
meditation17.php.
27. Miller, "What Makes a Good Life?"
28. Kent Dunnington, *Addiction and Virtue: Beyond the Models of Disease and
Choice* (Downers Grove: IVP, 2011), loc. 1194. Kindle.
29. *Yeldall Manor Newsletter*, Autumn 2011.
30. Ann Marlowe, *How to Stop Time: Heroin from A to Z* (New York: Basic
Books, 1999), 140,179. Kindle.
31. Bruce Alexander, *The Globalization of Addiction: A Study in Poverty of the
Spirit* (Oxford: Oxford University Press, 2008), 58.
32. Ibid., 60.
33. Johann Hari, *Chasing the Scream: The First and Last Days of the War on Drugs*
(London: Bloomsbury, 2015), loc. 3342. Kindle.
34. Steve Bruce, *God is Dead* (Oxford: Wiley-Blackwell, 2002), 2.
35. Bruce Alexander, *The Globalization of Addiction*, 3.
36. Alexander quoted by Johann Hari, *Chasing the Scream: The First and Last
Days of the War on Drugs* (London: Bloomsbury, 2015), loc. 3444. Kindle.
37. Judith Grisel, *Never Enough: The Neuroscience and Experience of Addiction*
(New York: Anchor Books, 2019), 7, 17. Kindle.
38. Russell Brand, *Recovery: Freedom from Our Addictions* (London: Bluebird,
2017), 15. Kindle.

Chapter 5: Enslaving Solution

1. Brian S. Catcher, "Benjamin Rush's Educational Campaign against Hard
Drinking," *American Journal of Public Health*, February 1993, Vol. 83, No. 2.
ncbi.nlm.nih.gov/pmc/articles/PMC1694575/pdf/amjph00526-0115.pdf.
2. Kent Dunnington, *Addiction and Virtue: Beyond the Models of Disease and
Choice* (Downers Grove: IVP, 2011), loc. 985. Kindle.
3. Catcher, "Benjamin Rush's Educational Campaign . . ."
4. Dunnington, *Addiction and Virtue*, 983.
5. Richard Rosenthal and Suzanne B Faris, "The etymology and early history of
'addiction.'" *Addiction Research & Theory*, 27:5, 2019, 439–442. tandfonline.
com/doi/pdf/10.1080/16066359.2018.1543412?needAccess=true.
6. Ibid., 439–440.
7. Ibid., 442.
8. Ibid., 438.
9. The most widely recognized being the American Psychiatric Association's
Diagnostic and Statistical Manual of Mental Disorders and the World Health

Organization's *International Statistical Classification of Diseases and Related Health Problems.*

10. Robert West and Jamie Brown, *Theory of Addiction* (Chichester: Wiley Blackwell, 2013), 10.

11. Ibid., 229.

12. Ibid., 20.

13. Bruce Alexander, *The Globalization of Addiction: A Study in Poverty of the Spirit* (Oxford: Oxford University Press, 2008), 35.

14. West and Brown, *Theory of Addiction*, 229.

15. Ibid., 7.

16. Judith Grisel, *Never Enough: The Neuroscience and Experience of Addiction* (New York: Anchor Books, 2019), 13. Kindle.

17. West and Brown, *Theory of Addiction*, 8.

18. Ibid., 8.

19. Ibid., 7.

20. David Courtwright, *The Age of Addiction: How Bad Habits Became Big Business* (Cambridge: Harvard University Press, 2019), loc. 85. Kindle.

21. Stanton Peele, *The Addiction Experience* (Center City: Hazelden, 1977), 273. Kindle.

22. Grisel, *Never Enough*, 1.

23. World Health Organization, "Global Status Report on Alcohol and Health 2018," 39, 72. apps.who.int/iris/bitstream/handle/10665/274603/9789241565639-eng .pdf.

24. Carl Hart, *High Price: Drugs, Neuroscience and Discovering Myself* (New York: Harper Perennial, 2014), 13. Kindle.

25. "DSM-5 Criteria for Substance Use Disorders," gatewayfoundation.org/ addiction-blog/dsm-5-substance-use-disorder/.

26. Timothy McMahan King, *Addiction Nation: What the Opioid Crisis Reveals About Us* (Harrisonburg: Herald Press, 2019), loc. 2223. Kindle.

27. Gerald May, *Addiction and Grace: Love and Spirituality in the Healing of Addictions* (New York: HarperCollins, 1988), 38–39. Kindle.

28. Jim Orford, *Excessive Appetites: A Psychological View of Addictions* (Chichester: John Wiley & Sons, 2001), 87.

Chapter 6: Toxic Relationship

1. Caroline Knapp, *Drinking: A Love Story* (New York: Bantam Dell, 1996), 96. Kindle.

2. William Cope Moyers, *Broken: My Story of Addiction and Redemption* (New York: Penguin, 2006), 185.

3. Ann Marlowe, *How to Stop Time: Heroin from A to Z* (New York: Basic Books, 1999), 198–199. Kindle.

4. Gabor Maté, *In the Realm of Hungry Ghosts: Close Encounters with Addiction* (Berkeley: North Atlantic Books, 2008), loc. 562. Kindle.

5. US Rep. Shirley Chisholm, quoted in *The Improvement and Reform of Law Enforcement and Criminal Justice in the United States*, Hearings Before the

Select Committee on Crime, House of Representatives, Ninety-First Congress (Washington: US Government Printing Office, 1969), 793.

6. Judith Grisel, *Never Enough: The Neuroscience and Experience of Addiction* (New York: Anchor Books, 2019), 5–6. Kindle.

7. Marlowe, *How to Stop Time*, 10.

8. Kent Dunnington, "The Addict as Modern Prophet," The Gospel Coalition, October 2, 2014, thegospelcoalition.org/article/addict-as-modern-prophet.

9. Ibid.

10. Gerald May, *Addiction and Grace: Love and Spirituality in the Healing of Addictions* (New York: HarperCollins, 1988), 13–14. Kindle.

11. *Yeldall Manor Newsletter*, Autumn 2013.

Chapter 7: The Apparatus of Addiction

1. Margarette Driscoll, "Love Failed Our Addicted Son," *The Sunday Times*, August 7, 2011, thetimes.co.uk/article/love-failed-to-save-our-addict-son-h8dlzf0q78n.

2. Bill W., *Alcoholics Anonymous* (New York: Alcoholics Anonymous World Services, Inc.), reproduction of *The Big Book of Alcoholics Anonymous*, 1st and 2nd eds. (Renegade Press), loc. 4618. Kindle.

3. Saint Augustine, *The Confessions: A New Translation by Henry Chadwick* (Oxford: Oxford University Press, 1991), loc. 2432, 2228. Kindle.

4. Saint Augustine, *Confessions*, loc. 3008.

5. Marc Lewis, "Disease, Choice, or Self-Medication? Models and Metaphors for Addiction," Understanding Addiction, June 8, 2012, memoirsofanaddicted brain.com/connect/disease-choice-or-self-medication-models-and-metaphors-for-addiction/.

6. Marc Lewis, *The Biology of Desire: Why Addiction Is Not a Disease* (New York: PublicAffairs, 2015), loc. 39. Kindle.

7. Ibid.

8. Ibid., loc. 700.

9. Ibid., loc. 39.

10. Ann Graybiel, "The Basal Ganglia: Learning New Tricks and Loving It," *Current Opinion in Neurobiology* 15 (2005): 638–44 cited by Charles Duhigg, *The Power of Habit: Why We Do What We Do in Life and Business* (New York: Random House, 2012), 20. Kindle.

11. Marc Lewis, *The Biology of Desire*, 300–301.

12. Charles Duhigg, *The Power of Habit: Why We Do What We Do in Life and Business* (New York: Random House, 2012), 20. Kindle.

13. Robert West and Jamie Brown, *Theory of Addiction* (Chichester: Wiley Blackwell, 2013), 174.

14. Lewis, *The Biology of Desire*, loc. 2814, 2848.

15. David Edmonds, "The Science of Addiction: Do You Always Like the Things You Want?," *BBC* News, December 12, 2020, bbc.com/news/stories-55221825.

16. Ibid.

17. Gabor Maté, *In the Realm of Hungry Ghosts: Close Encounters with Addiction* (Berkeley: North Atlantic Books, 2008), loc. 1818. Kindle.

Chapter 8: I Can't, But We Can

1. Interviews with Huseyin Djemil, June 8, 2021, and June 24, 2021.
2. Recovery Research Institute, "1 in 10 Americans Report Having Resolved a Significant Substance Problem," recoveryanswers.org/research-post/1-in-10-americans-report-having-resolved-a-significant-substance-use-problem/, citing Kelly, J. F., Bergman, B. G., Hoeppner, B. B., Vilsaint, C. L., and White, W. L. (2017). Prevalence and pathways of recovery from drug and alcohol problems in the United States population: Implications for practice, research, and policy. *Drug and Alcohol Dependence, 181* (Supplement C), 162–169.
3. samhsa.gov/sites/default/files/samhsa-recovery-5-6-14.pdf.
4. Gerald May, *Addiction and Grace: Love and Spirituality in the Healing of Addictions* (New York: HarperCollins, 1988), 14. Kindle.
5. Kent Dunnington, *Addiction and Virtue: Beyond the Models of Disease and Choice* (Downers Grove: IVP, 2011), loc. 475. Kindle.
6. Recovery Research Institute, "1 in 10 Americans," *Drug and Alcohol Dependence, 181*, 162-169.
7. Marc Lewis, *The Biology of Desire* (New York: PublicAffairs, 2015), loc. 427. Kindle.
8. Recovery Research Institute, "1 in 10 Americans report having resolved a significant substance problem," recoveryanswers.org/research-post/1-in-10-americans-report-having-resolved-a-significant-substance-use-problem/ citing Kelly, J. F., Bergman, B. G., Hoeppner, B. B., Vilsaint, C. L., and White, W. L. (2017). Prevalence and pathways of recovery from drug and alcohol problems in the United States population: Implications for practice, research, and policy. Drug and Alcohol Dependence, 181 (Supplement C), 162–69.
9. Gabor Maté, *In the Realm of Hungry Ghosts: Close Encounters with Addiction* (Berkeley: North Atlantic Books, 2008), loc. 4634. Kindle.
10. Ibid.
11. Robert West and Jamie Brown, *Theory of Addiction* (Chichester: Wiley Blackwell, 2013), 229.
12. Adam Alter, *Irresistible: Why We Can't Stop Checking, Scrolling, Clicking and Watching* (London: Vintage, 2017), 87. Kindle.
13. West and Brown, *Theory of Addiction*, 229.
14. Marc Lewis, *The Biology of Desire* (New York: PublicAffairs, 2015), loc. 1420. Kindle.
15. May, *Addiction and Grace*, 16.
16. samhsa.gov/medication-assisted-treatment.
17. Seth Haines, *Coming Clean: A Story of Faith* (Grand Rapids: Zondervan, 2015), 71. Kindle.
18. Lucy Foulkes, *Losing Our Minds: What Mental Illness Really Is and What It Isn't* (UK: Vintage, 2021), 188.
19. Isaac Chotiner, "A Sociologist of Religion on Protestants, Porn, and the Purity Industrial Complex,'" *The New Yorker*, May 3, 2019, newyorker.com/culture/q-and-a/a-sociologist-of-religion-on-protestants-porn-and-the-purity-industrial-complex.

20. Robert Granfield and William Cloud, *Coming Clean: Overcoming Addiction Without Treatment* (New York: New York University Press, 1999), loc. 2586. Kindle.
21. William White and William Cloud, "Recovery Capital: A Primer for Addictions Professionals," *Counselor,* 9(5), 22–27. naadac.org/assets/2416/whitewlcloudw2008_recovery_capital_a_primer.pdf.
22. Ibid.
23. Bruce Alexander, *The Globalization of Addiction: A Study in Poverty of the Spirit* (Oxford: Oxford University Press, 2008), 340.
24. Marc Lewis, *The Biology of Desire* (New York: PublicAffairs, 2015), loc. 2960. Kindle.
25. Lewis, *The Biology of Desire,* loc. 2960.
26. Maté, *In the Realm of Hungry Ghosts,* loc. 4802.
27. Lewis, *The Biology of Desire,* loc. 3016. Kindle.
28. Stanton Peele, *The Addiction Experience* (Center City: Hazelden, 1977), loc. 457. Kindle.

Chapter 9: Beyond Batman

1. Teun's photo documentary can be viewed at teunvoeten.com/photography/skid-row-crystal-meth.html.
2. Teun Voeten, "Skid Row: Inside the Epicentre of LA's Homeless and Crystal Meth Crisis," *The Independent,* October 10, 2021, independent.co.uk/arts-entertainment/photography/skid-row-la-homeless-crystal-meth-crisis-b1934786.html.
3. therowchurch.com/_make.
4. therowchurch.com/plan_a_visit.
5. therowchurch.com/_make.
6. I owe Dr. Conrad Gempf, Lecturer in New Testament at London School of Theology, for introducing me to the illustrative power of the Batman and Spider-Man distinction.
7. N. T. Wright, "City on a Hill", sermon at Durham Cathedral, October 17, 2006, ntwrightpage.com/2016/03/30/city-on-a-hill/.
8. *Yeldall Manor Newsletter,* Summer 2012.
9. Kenneth Bailey, *Poet & Peasant: A Literary-Cultural Approach to the Parables in Luke* (Grand Rapids: Eerdmans, 2000), 181–82.
10. Ibid., 185–187.
11. Craig Blomberg, *Interpreting the Parables* (Downers Grove: IVP, 1990), 176.
12. Private message shared on social media.
13. *Yeldall Manor Newsletter,* Autumn 2011.
14. John Mark Comer, *The Ruthless Elimination of Hurry* (Colorado Springs: Waterbrook, 2019), 76. Kindle.
15. Quoted by David Fitch, twitter.com/fitchest/status/1288470902016016386.
16. Comer, *The Ruthless Elimination of Hurry,* 84. Kindle.
17. Ibid., 87–88.

NOTES

Chapter 10: Rat Park Church

1. Aaron White, *Recovering: From Brokenness and Addiction to Blessedness and Community* (Grand Rapids: Baker Academic, 2020), 19, 14. Kindle.
2. Dallas Willard, *The Spirit of the Disciplines: Understanding How God Changes Lives* (New York: HarperCollins, 1999), 68. Kindle.
3. Seth Haines, *Coming Clean: A Story of Faith* (Grand Rapids: Zondervan, 2015), 118–119. Kindle.
4. Caroline Tisdale, "90 Meetings in 90 Days . . . It's Not Just for Newcomers," Fellowship Hall, August 1, 2021, fellowshiphall.com/2021/08/90-meetings-in-90-days-its-not-just-for-newcomers/.
5. White, *Recovering*, loc. 43. Kindle.
6. Kent Dunnington, "Small Groups Anonymous," *Christianity Today*, May 2019, 51–55.
7. Ibid.
8. Ibid.
9. Ibid.
10. Ibid.
11. Kent Dunnington, *Addiction and Virtue: Beyond the Models of Disease and Choice* (Downers Grove: IVP, 2011), 980, 1237. Kindle.
12. Kent Dunnington, "The Addict as Modern Prophet," The Gospel Coalition, October 2, 2014, thegospelcoalition.org/article/addict-as-modern-prophet.
13. Ibid.
14. Ibid.

Conclusion: Together in the Wilderness

1. Eyder Peralta, "Nicaragua Follows Its Own Path in Dealing with Drug Traffickers," NPR, October 26, 2014, npr.org/sections/parallels/2014/10/26/357791551/nicaragua-follows-its-own-path-in-dealing-with-drug-traffickers.
2. Bernd Debusmann, "Cocaine is King on Nicaragua's Caribbean Coast," *Reuters*, January 30, 2007, reuters.com/article/us-nicaragua-cocaine-idUSN2326993620070130.
3. Ibid.
4. Ibid.
5. Kosuke Koyama, *Three Mile An Hour God* (London: SCM Press, 1979), 6–7.
6. Timothy McMahan King, *Addiction Nation: What the Opioid Crisis Reveals About Us* (Harrisonburg: Herald Press, 2019), 175.
7. Deborah and David Beddoe, *The Heart of Recovery: How Compassion and Community Offer Hope in the Wake of Addiction* (Grand Rapids: Revell, 2019), 14–15.
8. Martin Heidegger summarised by Francis Seeburger, *Addiction and Responsibility: An Enquiry Into the Addictive Mind* (New York: Crossroad, 1993), loc. 1682.
9. Deborah and David Beddoe, *The Heart of Recovery*, 12.

205

About the Author

Andy Partington leads the work of Novō Communities and Novō Adventures.

Novō Communities' vision is to bring new life to individuals, peace to families, and hope to communities gripped by addiction by empowering local teams in developing nations to create transformational communities that offer healing, wholeness, and hope.

Novō Adventures, a motorcycle tour operator, is a social enterprise that generates income to support the work of Novō Communities.

Andy has served as Director of Training at London School of Theology, in local church leadership in the UK and Bolivia, and as CEO of Yeldall Manor, an addiction treatment center in the southeast of England. Andy's doctoral dissertation—published as *Church and State*—explored the role of the Church of England bishops in the House of Lords.

Andy is married to Mickey and is the proud father of Daniel, Jemimah, Phoebe, JJ, and Miah.

You can learn more about the work of Novō
at novocommunities.org and novoadventures.com.